HOW TO PASS

STANDARD GRADE
MUSIC

Joe McGowan

HODDER
GIBSON
PART OF HACHETTE LIVRE UK

D0543299

If the CD is missing from this package, please contact us on 0141 848 1609 or at hoddergibson@hodder.co.uk, advising where and when you purchased the book.

Although every effort has been made to ensure that website addresses are correct at time of going to press, Hodder Gibson cannot be held responsible for the content of any website mentioned in this book. It is sometimes possible to find a relocated web page by typing in the address of the home page for a website in the URL window of your browser.

Papers used in this book are natural, renewable and recyclable products. They are made from wood grown in sustainable forests. The logging and manufacturing processes conform to the environmental regulations of the country of origin.

Orders: please contact Bookpoint Ltd, 130 Milton Park, Abingdon, Oxon OX14 4SB. Telephone: (44) 01235 827720. Fax: (44) 01235 400454. Lines are open from 9.00–5.00, Monday to Saturday, with a 24-hour message answering service. Visit our website at www.hoddereducation.co.uk. Hodder Gibson can be contacted direct on: Tel: 0141 848 1609; Fax: 0141 889 6315; email: hoddergibson@hodder.co.uk

© Joe McGowan 2005
First published in 2005 by
Hodder Gibson, an imprint of Hodder Education, part of Hachette Livre UK
2a Christie Street
Paisley PA1 1NB

Impression number   10 9 8 7 6 5 4 3

Year   2010   2009   2008

Cover photo from Image Bank/Getty Images
Typeset in 10.5 on 14pt Frutiger Light by Phoenix Photosetting, Chatham, Kent
Printed and bound in Great Britain by Martins The Printers, Berwick-upon-Tweed

A catalogue record for this title is available from the British Library

ISBN-13: 978-0-340-88795-0

CONTENTS

Acknowledgements

Special thanks to Ann-Marie Crombie, Janet Young (Stonelaw High School), Graham and Evelyn Laurie (The Graham Laurie School of Music), Allan McKechnie, David Brockett, Jon Paul McMillan and everyone at Hodder Gibson.

The publishers would like to thank the following for permission to reproduce copyright material:

Cartoons © Moira Munro 2005.

Lyric acknowledgements

Shine On Ruby Mountain. Words and Music by Kenny Young © 1970 Kangaroo Music Inc, USA. EMI Songs Ltd, London WC2H 0QY. Reproduced by permission of International Music Publications Ltd (a trading name of Faber Music Ltd). All Rights Reserved. Ruby, Don't Take Your Love To Town. Words & Music by Mel Tillis © Copyright 1966 Cedarwood Publishing Company Incorporated, USA. Universal Music Publishing Limited. All Rights Reserved. International Copyright Secured; Angels. Words & Music by Robbie Williams & Guy Chambers © Copyright 1997 EMI Virgin Music Limited (50%)/BMG Music Publishing Limited (50%). Used by permission of Music Sales Limited. All Rights Reserved. International Copyright Secured; Angels. Words and Music by Robbie Williams and Guy Chambers © 1997. EMI Virgin Music Ltd and BMG Music Publishing Ltd. (50%) EMI Virgin Music Ltd, London WC2H 0QY. Reproduced by permission of International Music Publications Ltd (a trading name of Faber Music Ltd.). All Rights Reserved. Flying Without Wings. Words & Music by Steve Mac & Wayne Hector © Copyright 1999 Rokstone Music (50%)/Rondor Music (London) Limited (50%). All Rights Reserved. International Copyright Secured. Published by Rokstone Music Ltd (50%); The Story of My Life. Words by Hal David, Music by Burt Bacharach. © Copyright 1957 Casa David Music Incorporated. Famous Music Corporation (50%)/Universal/MCA Music Limited (50%). Used by permission of Music Sales Limited. All Rights Reserved. International Copyright Secured.

CD credits

Tracks 1, 2, 3, 4, 16, 43, 45, 75, 76, 77 © Joe McGowan; Track 5 2/4 March (0.28). From the Recording 'Spirit of Scotland' on the Lochshore Label CDLOC 1087, KRL, Hillington Park, Glasgow; Track 11 My Bride To Be – Winston Samuels, from the original recording Trojan Ska Box Set Vol.2. Issued under licence from Sanctuary Records Group Ltd; Track 14 Heaven On My Mind – The Original Five Blind Boys of Alabama, taken from the original recording The Sermon. Used with permission of Ace Records Ltd; Track 21 The Shepherd of the Downs, released under license from Topic Records Ltd (www.topicrecords.co.uk); Track 22 One Day More – Schonberg/Boublil/Kretzmer/Natel, SDRM/Alain Boublil Overseas Ltd. 1995 Exallshow Limited; Track 24 "CARMEN: L'AMOUR EST UN OISEASU REBELLE (ACT 1)". Performed by LONDON SYMPHONY ORCHESTRA, Courtesy of Deutsche Grammophon, Part of the Universal Music Group; Track 25 THE ART OF FUGUE Bwv 1080: FUGA A 2 CLAVICEMBALI (RECTUS). Performed by KARL MUNCHINGER / STUTTGARTER KAMMERORCHESTER, Courtesy of The Decca Music Group, Part of the Universal Music Group; Track 27 Hey! Hey! Hey! Hey! – The Johnny Otis Orchestra, taken from the original recording Johnny Otis Rock 'n' Roll Hit Parade. Used with permission of Ace Records Ltd; Track 30 Spiral Staircase – Ralph McTell, from the original recording 'The Acoustic Folk Box'. Issued under licence from Sanctuary Records Group Ltd; Track 37 At My Front Door – The Jayos, taken from the original recording Johnny Otis Rock 'n' Roll Hit Parade. Used with permission of Ace Records Ltd; Track 39 "CARMEN: VOICI LA CLOCHE QUI SONNE, MON LIUTENANT LA CLOCHE A SONNE". Performed by LONDON SYMPHONY ORCHESTRA, Courtesy of Deutsche Grammophon, Part of the Universal Music Group; Tracks 44, 46 © David Brockett; Track 47 Jig (0.30). From the Recording 'Spirit of Scotland' on the Lochshore Label CDLOC 1087, KRL, Hillington Park, Glasgow; Track 48 "Look at Ewen's Coracle" – Annie Arnott. From the Greentrax album "Music From The Western Isles" – CDTRAX 9002. (P) 1992 Greentrax Recordings Ltd. Licensed to Hodder Gibson by Greentrax Recordings. www.greentrax.com; Track 54 "CARMEN: MONSIEUR LE BRIGADIER?". Performed by LONDON SYMPHONY ORCHESTRA, Courtesy of Deutsche Grammophon, Part of the Universal Music Group; Track 58 Piano Concerto in F Major (1st Movement). George Gershwin, from the album Piano Concerto in F Major. Used by kind permission of Pickwick Group Limited; Track 60 "CARMEN: VOICI LA CLOCHE QUI SONNE, MON LIUTENANT LA CLOCHE A SONNE". Performed by LONDON SYMPHONY ORCHESTRA, Courtesy of Deutsche Grammophon, Part of the Universal Music Group; Track 62 Soliloguy (Javert's Suicide), Schonberg/Boublil/Kretzmer/Natel, SDRM/Alain Boublil Overseas Ltd, 1995 Exallshow Limited; Track 63 Mattie Rag (AKA Old Matilda) – Lord Tanamo, from the original recording Trojan Ska Box Set Vol.2. Issued under licence from Sanctuary Records Group Ltd; Track 66 QE2/QE2 Finale – Mike Oldfield. (P) 1980 The copyright in this sound recording is owned by Virgin Records Ltd. Licensed courtesy of Virgin Records Limited; Track 70 William Tell Overture – Mike Oldfield. (P) 1976 The copyright in this sound recording is owned by Virgin Records Limited. Licensed courtesy of Virgin Records Limited.

Every effort has been made to trace all copyright holders for printed and audio material, but if any have been inadvertently overlooked the Publishers will be pleased to make the necessary arrangements at the first opportunity.

INTRODUCTION

Welcome to *How to Pass Standard Grade Music*!

If you are reading this I already know two things about you: one is that you enjoy music enough to want a respectable qualification in the subject; the other is that you are a sensible person, otherwise you wouldn't have bothered picking up this book in the first place.

So, now that we have established that you are smart *and* care about how well you do in Standard Grade Music, the next positive step you can take towards achieving your goal is to keep reading.

This revision guide book is designed to help you revise all the things you have already worked on in class, and review what you need to know in order to prepare for the Standard Grade Music exams and assessments. But you shouldn't just think of this as a book that you will only need to use when the exams get closer; *How to Pass Standard Grade Music* can also help you as you progress through your course, because it is full of exercises involving musical concepts, listening and inventing, as well as handy tips and advice along the way – in other words, loads of things that will show you how to pass!

THE STANDARD GRADE MUSIC QUALIFICATION

The aim of Standard Grade Music is to give you experience in each of the three main areas of musical activity: **Listening**, **Inventing**, and **Performing**. Knowledge of these will lead to a greater understanding and enjoyment of music.

In order to receive your qualification, you will be assessed in these three different areas, each of which will be given a separate mark that will then be added together to determine your final grade.

Listening

During your course you will listen to lots of different kinds of music and learn about the elements (or concepts) that go into putting it together. Your assessment in this component will be a Listening test based upon various musical excerpts on which you will answer mainly multiple-choice questions. The Listening test will last between about 45 minutes and 1 hour 45 minutes, depending on whether you are at Foundation, General or Credit level in Listening.

Inventing

There are three activities in this area: **Composing**, **Improvising** and **Arranging**. Throughout your course you will create new music (composing), learn how to invent music on the spot (improvising), and alter an existing piece of music by changing something about it (arranging). Your work in these three activities (recordings, written or printed music etc.) will be assessed by your teacher.

Performing

In this part you are required to play **two** different instruments. You will have the choice to play solo on both instruments, or solo on one instrument and as a member of a group on the other.

Solo Performing

Here you will play a selection of contrasting music, lasting between four and six minutes in total (on each instrument), which you will have prepared on an instrument (which can include voice) of your choice. Your performance on **one** instrument will be assessed by your class teacher, the other in the presence of a visiting examiner who will visit your school in February or March of the exam year. Your grade will depend upon the standard of the music you choose for each instrument and how well you play.

Group Performing

If you choose this option, during your course you will experience playing various kinds of music as a member of a group consisting of you and one or more fellow students. You could, for example, be the bass guitarist or drummer in a pop or rock group, or the clarinettist in a keyboard and clarinet duo. Your music teacher will guide you, and continuously assess your work in this area – which will include recording some of your performances on a *different* instrument to that chosen for your **Solo Performing** test. Your best performances/recordings will decide your final grade. (Recordings of your group performances have to be completed by April of the exam year.)

Each of the above components of the Standard Grade Music qualification are assessed at either Foundation, General or Credit level, with Credit level requiring the greatest knowledge or skill. Students can be assessed at different levels for each component; this allows everyone to reach their highest level of achievement in the three components without feeling pressurised to maintain a particular standard in each.

HOW TO USE THIS BOOK

You can work through the revision exercises in this book in any order you choose, depending on your ability level in each section, but you might find it helpful to complete Chapter 1 first, as it contains information relevant to all other sections in the book. In any case, you will probably need to keep referring back to Chapter 1 as you progress.

There are **four** different kinds of revision exercise used in this book:

Ten-Minute Testers

These require you to jot down (in note form, not sentences) as much information as you can on particular concepts in about ten minutes. They will show you how much you can remember (or have forgotten!), and therefore what you might need to revise more carefully. The Ten-Minute Testers should also improve your ability to recall information quickly when you need to – like in an exam.

'For Practice' exercises

These will present you with specific tasks which will test your knowledge or skill in a particular area (or give you some extra practice with it), as well as ensure that you fully understand the material you are revising.

Buddy Study

Two heads are better than one! With 'Buddy Study' you will tackle a set task or exercise with another Standard Grade Music student (or students), the important thing being that together you share and discuss a musical activity and benefit from each other's input – and enjoy all of it!

CD-based exercises and examples

This book comes with a CD containing musical excerpts and examples which you will need to listen to in order to respond to the revision questions etc. The track that you need to listen to in relation to a question or exercise will be clearly indicated in the text.

Extra help

Hints and Tips

'Hints and Tips' appear here and there throughout the book containing brief facts, tips and other bits of helpful and important information for you to note.

Reference pages

Reference pages are included which contain important musical information at a glance.

Glossary of musical concepts

The Glossary contains brief definitions of all the concepts you need to know at Foundation, General and Credit levels. You can use the glossary for reference and memory-jogging if you have forgotten the meaning of a musical word or concept.

But before we begin ...

Before starting your revision, you should **gather together all your course work** (notes, worksheets and so on) and put it in an order which allows you to refer to it quickly as you work through this book. For example, you might put the material into categories under headings such as 'Scottish music', 'Jazz', 'Folk music', 'Inventing' etc. so that all the information you have on a particular topic can be found easily as you attempt the exercises.

If you are a neat, well-organised person, you may already have your work categorised and in good order, but if your music folder currently resembles the lid of an overflowing wheelie-bin on collection day then **get it sorted!**

Good organisation makes for easier, more effective revising and prevents wasting time wading through a messy folder whenever you want to find something. It will also help to motivate you in your revision work and cut down on stress and frustration, especially near exam time.

You might also find the following sources helpful as you work through this book:

◆ **www.sqa.org.uk** – the website of the Scottish Qualifications Authority – good for information on exams and publications

◆ **www.allmusic.com** – a website containing lots of information about all kinds of music and composers

◆ A good music dictionary – an invaluable source for looking up information on all aspects of music.

REVISING MUSICAL CONCEPTS

In this section you will be revising musical concepts. These are the various elements which distinguish one kind of music from another, and generally make all music what it is. There are many concepts, but each belongs in one of seven broad categories:

1 **Melody** (the tune or tunes in a piece of music)

2 **Rhythm** (the different time durations of musical notes combined together in a piece of music)

3 **Style** (the different types of music – for example, rock, pop, folk, blues, Latin-American)

4 **Timbre** (the different kinds of sounds that musical instruments – including voice – can produce both individually and when playing together in various combinations)

5 **Texture, Structure and Design** (the way different musical compositions are constructed, and the elements which are part of that construction)

6 **Harmony** (the notes and/or chords which accompany a melody)

7 **Dynamics** (the different volume levels in a piece of music).

In the following exercises you will revise the concepts within each of these categories. If you are currently at Foundation level you should focus on the Foundation level exercises; if you are at General level you should tackle **both** the Foundation and General level exercises, and Credit level students should work through **all three** exercise levels. (Write your answers in pencil, as any corrections can then be made more easily.)

You should not, however, be discouraged from attempting the higher level exercises if you are at Foundation or General level, since it is possible that you will have covered some more advanced work in class. Aiming higher will also help you to improve and get the best result from your current level.

Don't worry if the way you have been studying musical concepts in class doesn't quite match the following exercises, or if there are things which you haven't covered yet. Your teacher will have his or her own way of working and, if necessary, will advise you on how to work through each part of this book.

More exercises related to musical concepts can be found in Chapter 2, where you will have the opportunity to respond to the sorts of multiple-choice questions you will encounter in your Standard Grade Listening test.

Answers to the questions in this section are at the back of the book, and definitions of the musical concepts covered can be found in the Glossary of Musical Concepts on pages 99–117.

Concepts 1: Melody – Foundation level

At Foundation level you should know about:

- ascending and descending melody
- stepwise and leaping melody
- glissando (plural: glissandi)
- repetition
- theme

- question and answer
- section
- sequence
- contrast
- broken chord.

Ten-Minute Tester

Jot down what you already know about each of the melody concepts listed above. Revise any concepts you are unsure about before attempting Listening Exercises 1 and 2.

Listening Exercise 1: CD track 1

Read the questions below very carefully before listening to CD track 1. You can listen to the track more than once if you need to, but try to answer the questions after hearing it no more than **twice**.

Question 1. Listen to CD track 1 and tick **two** boxes which best describe the melody (remember to use a **pencil** for this).

- ☐ Leaping
- ☐ Moving by step
- ☐ Ascending
- ☐ Descending

Question 2. Listen to CD track 1 again and decide if there is a GLISSANDO present. Tick **one** box.

The excerpt has a glissando. ☐ TRUE **or** ☐ FALSE

Listening Exercise 2: CD track 2

Read the questions below very carefully before listening to CD track 2. Try to listen to the track no more than **twice** before answering the questions (once for each question).

Question 1. Listen to CD track 2 and tick the best description of a feature used in the *melody*. Tick **one** box.

☐ Repetition

☐ Question and Answer

Question 2. Listen to CD track 2 again and tick **one** box to describe a feature used in the music which *accompanies* the melody.

☐ Sequence

☐ Broken chords

Concepts 1: Melody – General level

Note: At General level, you should do the exercises for both Foundation and General levels.

The Melody concepts you need to know about at General Level are the same as those for Foundation Level *plus*:

◆ phrase

◆ imitation

◆ variation

◆ ornament

◆ scales: major, minor, chromatic, diatonic, whole-tone, pentatonic, blues

◆ grace note.

Ten-Minute Tester

Jot down what you already know about each of the melody concepts listed above. Revise any concepts you are unsure about before attempting Listening Exercise 3.

Listening Exercise 3: CD track 3

Read the questions below very carefully before listening to CD track 3. Try to answer the questions after hearing the track no more than **twice** (once for each question).

Question 1. Listen to CD track 3 and tick **one** box to describe a feature used in the excerpt.

☐ Imitation

☐ Grace notes

☐ Variation

Question 2. Listen to CD track 3 again and tick **one** box to describe the type of scale you hear.

☐ Major

☐ Minor

☐ Chromatic

☐ Pentatonic

☐ Whole-tone

Concepts 1: Melody – Credit level

Note: At Credit level, you should also work through the exercises for both Foundation and General levels.

The melody concepts you need to know about at Credit level are the same as those for both Foundation and General levels *plus*:

◆ relative major and minor

◆ modal, tonal and atonal music

◆ semitone and tone

◆ modulation

◆ contrary motion

◆ interval

◆ inversion

◆ register.

Ten-Minute Tester

Jot down what you already know about each of the melody concepts listed above. Revise any concepts you are unsure about before attempting Listening Exercise 4.

Listening Exercise 4: CD track 4

Read the questions below very carefully before listening to CD track 4. Try to answer the questions after hearing the track no more than **four** times (once for each question).

Question 1. Listen to CD track 4 and tick **one** box which describes the melody.

☐ Tonal

☐ Atonal

☐ Modal

Question 2. Listen to CD track 4 again and decide if the melody is in a **high** or **low** Register. Tick **one** box.

☐ The melody is in a **high register**

☐ The melody is in a **low register**

Question 3. Listen to CD track 4 again and tick **one** box to describe what you hear.

☐ The music modulates from the **minor** key into its **relative major** key

☐ The music modulates from the **major** key into its **relative minor** key

☐ The music is **modal** and there is no key change

☐ The music is **atonal** and there is no key change

Question 4. Listen to CD track 4 once more and decide if the accompaniment moves in **similar motion** or **contrary motion** to the melody. Tick **one** box.

☐ The accompaniment moves in SIMILAR MOTION

☐ The accompaniment moves in CONTRARY MOTION

Concepts 2: Rhythm – Foundation level

At Foundation level you should know about:

- accent
- accented
- rhythm (slower and faster rhythms)
- beat
- bar (2, 3 and 4 beats per bar)
- syncopation
- march
- strathspey
- reel
- jig
- waltz
- pause (fermata)
- *a tempo*
- on the beat
- off the beat.

Ten-Minute Tester

Jot down what you already know about each of the rhythm concepts listed above. Revise any concepts you are unsure about before attempting Listening Exercises 5 and 6.

Listening Exercise 5: CD track 5

Read the following questions very carefully before listening to CD track 5. Try to answer the questions after hearing the recorded excerpt no more than **twice** (once for each question).

Question 1. Listen to CD track 5 and decide if there are TWO beats, THREE beats, or FOUR beats in the bar. Tick **one** box.

☐ Two beats in the bar

☐ Three beats in the bar

☐ Four beats in the bar

Question 2. Listen to CD track 5 again and tick the correct description of what you hear. Tick **one** box.

☐ Waltz

☐ Reel

☐ March

☐ Jig

Listening Exercise 6: CD track 6

Read the questions below very carefully before listening to CD track 6. Try to answer the questions after hearing the recorded excerpt no more than **twice** (once for each question).

Question 1. Listen to CD track 6 and tick **one** box to describe what you hear.

☐ The accent is on the beat

☐ The accent is off the beat (syncopation)

Question 2. Listen to CD track 6 again and tick **one** box to describe a feature in the music.

☐ Repetition

☐ Pause (fermata)

☐ Goes back to its original speed (*a tempo*) after changing speed briefly

Concepts 2: Rhythm – General level

The Rhythm concepts you need to know about at General level are the same as those for Foundation level *plus*:

- simple time
- compound time
- unaccented
- upbeat
- downbeat
- anacrusis
- lead-in
- speed variations
- Scotch snap
- sforzando.

Ten-Minute Tester

Jot down what you already know about each of the rhythm concepts listed on page 11. Revise any concepts you are unsure about before attempting Listening Exercises 7 and 8.

Listening Exercise 7: CD track 7

Read the questions below very carefully before listening to CD track 7. Try to answer the questions after hearing the recorded excerpt no more than **twice** (once for each question).

Question 1. Listen to CD track 7 and decide if the excerpt is in SIMPLE TIME or COMPOUND TIME. Tick **one** box.

☐ The excerpt is in SIMPLE TIME

☐ The excerpt is in COMPOUND TIME

Question 2. Listen to CD track 7 again and identify **two** features present. Tick **two** boxes.

☐ Lead-in

☐ Scotch snap

☐ Sforzando chords

☐ Anacrusis

Listening Exercise 8: CD track 8

Read the questions below very carefully before listening to CD track 8. Try to answer the questions after hearing the recorded excerpt no more than **twice** (once for each question).

Question 1. Listen to CD track 8 and tick **one** box to describe what you hear.

☐ The downbeats are accented

☐ The upbeats are accented (syncopation)

☐ Sometimes the downbeats are accented, and sometimes the upbeats are accented

☐ The beats are unaccented

Question 2. Which of the following is a feature in the extract? Tick **one** box.

☐ Accelerando (*accel.*)

☐ Ritardando (*rit.*)

☐ Rubato

Concepts 2: Rhythm – Credit level

The rhythm concepts you need to know about at Credit level are the same as those for both Foundation and General levels *plus*:

◆ rhythmic groupings in simple and compound time

◆ cross rhythms.

Ten-Minute Tester

Jot down what you already know about each of the rhythm concepts listed above. Revise any concepts you are unsure about before attempting Listening Exercise 9.

Listening Exercise 9: CD track 9

Read the questions below very carefully before listening to CD track 9. Try to answer the questions after hearing the recorded excerpt no more than **three** times (once for each question). You might find the reference section on time signatures and rhythmic groupings on pages 93–94 helpful for this exercise.

Question 1. Listen to CD track 9 and identify the time signature. Tick **one** box.

☐ 3/4 time (simple triple time)

☐ 6/8 time (compound duple time)

☐ 4/4 time (simple quadruple time)

Question 2. Listen to CD track 9 again and tick **one** box to describe the rhythms in this excerpt.

☐ The music moves mostly in DOTTED CROTCHETS and QUAVERS

☐ The music moves mostly in QUAVERS and SEMIQUAVERS

Question 3. Listen to CD track 9 once more and decide if the excerpt contains cross rhythms. Tick **one** box.

The excerpt contains cross rhythms. ☐ TRUE **or** ☐ FALSE

Concepts 3: Style – Foundation level

At Foundation level you should know about:

◆ pop
◆ swing

◆ rock
◆ Negro spiritual

◆ rock 'n' roll
◆ jazz

◆ reggae
◆ blues

- ◆ Latin-American
- ◆ ragtime

- ◆ Scottish
- ◆ folk.

Ten-Minute Tester

Jot down what you already know about each of the style concepts listed above. Revise any concepts you are unsure about before attempting Listening Exercises 10 and 11.

Listening Exercise 10: CD track 10

Read the question below very carefully before listening to CD track 10. Try to answer the question after listening to the recorded excerpt no more than **once**.

Question 1. Listen to CD track 10 and identify the musical style. Tick **one** box.

- ☐ Pop
- ☐ Latin-American
- ☐ Blues
- ☐ Folk
- ☐ Rock
- ☐ Swing

Listening Exercise 11: CD track 11

Read the question below very carefully before listening to CD track 11. Try to answer the question after listening to the recorded excerpt no more than **once**.

Question 1. Listen to CD track 11 and identify the musical style. Tick **one** box.

- ☐ Rock 'n' Roll
- ☐ Reggae
- ☐ Ragtime
- ☐ Jazz
- ☐ Negro spiritual

Concepts 3: Style – General level

The features of style you need to know about at General level are the same as those for Foundation level *plus*:

- ◆ baroque
- ◆ samba

- ◆ Dixieland
- ◆ 'scat' singing

◆ salsa

◆ vamp.

◆ romantic

Ten-Minute Tester

Jot down what you already know about each of the style concepts listed above. Revise any concepts you are unsure about before attempting Listening Exercises 12 and 13.

Listening Exercise 12: CD track 12

Read the questions below very carefully before listening to CD track 12. Try to answer the questions after hearing the recorded excerpt no more than **twice** (once for each question).

Question 1. Listen to CD track 12 and identify the musical style. Tick **one** box.

☐ Samba

☐ Salsa

☐ Dixieland

☐ Romantic

Question 2. Listen to CD track 12 again and decide if the excerpt is an example of scat singing. Tick **one** box.

The excerpt is an example of scat singing. ☐ TRUE **or** ☐ FALSE

Listening Exercise 13: CD track 13

Read the questions below very carefully before listening to CD track 13. Try to answer the questions after hearing the recorded extract no more than **twice** (once for each question).

Question 1. Listen to CD track 13 and identify **two** features of the music. Tick **two** boxes.

☐ The structure of the music is more obvious than its drama

☐ Brass and percussion instruments have an important role in the orchestra

☐ The mood or emotion is expressed very powerfully

☐ Vamp

Question 2. Based on your answers to Question 1 above, do you think the excerpt is a good example of Romantic music? Tick **one** box.

The excerpt is a good example of ROMANTIC music. ☐ TRUE **or** ☐ FALSE

Concepts 3: Style – Credit level

The style concepts you need to know about at Credit level are the same as those for both Foundation and General levels *plus*:

- aleatoric
- boogie-woogie
- classical
- minimalist
- soul music
- impressionism
- neo-classical

- serialism
- gospel
- musique concrète
- Passion
- country
- Indian
- atonal

Ten-Minute Tester

Jot down what you already know about each of the style concepts listed above. Revise any concepts you are unsure about before attempting Listening Exercises 14, 15 and 16.

Listening Exercise 14: CD track 14

Read the question below very carefully before listening to CD track 14. Try to answer the question after hearing the recorded excerpt no more than **once**.

Question 1. Listen to CD track 14 and identify the musical style. Tick **one** box.

- ☐ Boogie-woogie
- ☐ Soul music
- ☐ Country
- ☐ Gospel
- ☐ Aleatoric

Listening Exercise 15: CD track 15

Read the question below very carefully before listening to CD track 15. Try to answer the question after hearing the recorded extract no more than **once**.

Question 1. Listen to CD track 15 and identify the musical style. Tick **one** box.

- ☐ Impressionism
- ☐ Serialism
- ☐ Passion
- ☐ Classical
- ☐ Minimalist

Chapter 1

Listening Exercise 16: CD track 16

Read the question below very carefully before listening to CD track 16. Try to answer the question after hearing the recorded excerpt no more than **once**.

Question 1. Listen to CD track 16 and identify the musical style. Tick **one** box.

☐ Indian

☐ Neo-classical

☐ Atonal

☐ Musique concrète

Concepts 4: Timbre – Foundation level

At Foundation level you should know about:

- staccato
- legato
- double stopping
- sound
- silence
- sustained
- striking
- blowing
- bowing
- strumming
- plucking
- slapping
- muted/muting
- orchestra (woodwind, brass, percussion, strings)
- pipe band
- wind/military band
- brass band
- steel band
- big band
- Scottish dance band
- pop group
- folk group
- rock group
- jazz group
- acoustic
- recorders
- keyboards
- guitars (acoustic and electric)
- fiddle
- organ
- drum fill
- vocal/choral music
- lead vocals
- backing vocals.

Ten-Minute Tester

Jot down what you already know about each of the timbre concepts listed on page 17. If you are unsure about any of the concepts revise them thoroughly before attempting Listening Exercises 17 and 18.

Listening Exercise 17: CD track 17

Read the questions below very carefully before listening to CD track 17. Try to answer the questions after listening to the recorded excerpt no more than **three** times (once for each question).

Question 1. Listen to CD track 17 and identify the type of group playing. Tick **one** box.

☐ Folk group

☐ Rock group

☐ Pop group

☐ Jazz group

☐ Orchestra

Question 2. Listen to CD track 17 again and identify the solo instrument you hear playing. Tick **one** box.

☐ Guitar

☐ Keyboard

☐ Trumpet

☐ Recorder

☐ Clarinet

Question 3. Listen to CD track 17 once more and identify how the solo instrument plays the melody. Tick **one** box.

☐ The melody is played STACCATO

☐ The melody is played LEGATO

Listening Exercise 18: CD track 18

Read the following questions very carefully before listening to CD track 18. Try to answer the questions after hearing the recorded excerpt no more than **twice** (once for each question).

Question 1. Listen to CD track 18 and identify the type of band playing. Tick **one** box.

☐ Wind/military band

☐ Brass band

☐ Big band

☐ Steel band

☐ Scottish dance band

☐ Pipe band

Question 2. Listen to CD track 18 again and tick **one** box to describe how the instruments play the melody.

☐ Bowing

☐ Striking

☐ Blowing

☐ Plucking

Concepts 4: Timbre – General level

The timbre concepts you need to know about at General level are the same as those for Foundation level *plus*:

- Indonesian music
- gamelan music
- Ghanaian drum ensemble
- Latin percussion group
- voice (soprano, alto, tenor, bass)
- orchestral, keyboard and folk instruments

- drone
- electronic music
- delay
- distortion
- reverb
- electric drums.

Ten-Minute Tester

Jot down what you already know about each of the timbre concepts listed above. Revise any concepts you are unsure about before attempting Listening Exercise 19.

Listening Exercise 19: CD track 19

Read the following questions very carefully before listening to CD track 19. Try to answer the questions after hearing the recorded excerpt no more than **three** times (once for each question).

Question 1. Listen to CD track 19 and identify the type of group playing. Tick **one** box.

- ☐ Gamelan
- ☐ Latin percussion group
- ☐ Ghanaian drum ensemble
- ☐ Orchestra

Question 2. Listen to CD track 19 again and identify the solo instrument you hear playing. Tick **one** box.

- ☐ Trumpet
- ☐ Clarinet
- ☐ Flute
- ☐ Saxophone

Question 3. Listen to CD track 19 once more and identify another instrument you hear playing in the group.

- ☐ Trumpet
- ☐ Clarinet
- ☐ Slide guitar
- ☐ Synthesiser

Concepts 4: Timbre – Credit level

The timbre concepts you need to know about at Credit level are the same as those for both Foundation and General levels *plus*:

- ◆ vibrato
- ◆ melismatic
- ◆ syllabic
- ◆ mezzo
- ◆ mezzo-soprano
- ◆ counter-tenor
- ◆ baritone
- ◆ con sordino
- ◆ flutter-tonguing
- ◆ col legno
- ◆ arco
- ◆ pizzicato
- ◆ trill
- ◆ tremolando/tremolo
- ◆ a cappella
- ◆ chamber music
- ◆ Sprechgesang.

Ten-Minute Tester

Jot down what you already know about each of the timbre concepts listed above. Revise any concepts you are unsure about before attempting Listening Exercise 20.

Listening Exercise 20: CD track 20

Read the questions below very carefully before listening to CD track 20. Try to answer the questions after hearing the recorded excerpt no more than **three times** (once for each question).

Question 1. Listen to CD track 20 and tick **one** box to identify the kind of singing you hear.

- ☐ Melismatic
- ☐ Syllabic
- ☐ A cappella
- ☐ Sprechgesang

Question 2. Listen to CD track 20 again and identify the **highest** voice range you hear. Tick **one** box.

- ☐ Soprano
- ☐ Alto
- ☐ Counter-tenor
- ☐ Baritone

Question 3. Listen to CD track 20 one more time and tick **one** box to identify a feature in the STRING section of the orchestral accompaniment.

- ☐ Col legno
- ☐ Pizzicato
- ☐ Trill
- ☐ Tremolando/tremolo

Concepts 5: Texture, Structure and Design – Foundation level

At Foundation level you should know about:

- ◆ unison/octave
- ◆ harmony
- ◆ chord
- ◆ solo
- ◆ ensemble
- ◆ accompanied
- ◆ unaccompanied
- ◆ ostinato
- ◆ riff
- ◆ round
- ◆ theme and variations
- ◆ opera
- ◆ musical
- ◆ overture
- ◆ hymn tune
- ◆ traditional song.

Ten-Minute Tester

Jot down what you already know about each of the texture, structure and design concepts listed on page 21. If you are unsure about any of the concepts revise them thoroughly before attempting Listening Exercises 21 and 22.

Listening Exercise 21: CD track 21

Read the questions below very carefully before listening to CD track 21. Try to answer the questions after listening to the recorded excerpt no more than **twice** (once for each question).

Question 1. Listen to CD track 21 and tick **one** box to describe what you hear.

☐ Solo voice

☐ Voices in unison/octaves

☐ Voices in harmony

Question 2. Listen to CD track 21 again and decide if the voices are accompanied or unaccompanied. Tick **one** box.

☐ Accompanied

☐ Unaccompanied

Listening Exercise 22: CD track 22

Read the questions below very carefully before listening to CD track 22. Try to answer the questions after listening to the recorded excerpt no more than **twice** (once for each question).

Question 1. Listen to CD track 22 and tick **one** box to identify the type of piece you hear.

☐ Opera

☐ Musical

☐ Hymn tune

☐ Traditional song

Question 2. Listen to CD track 22 again and decide if there is an OSTINATO present. Tick **one** box.

The piece has an OSTINATO. ☐ TRUE **or** ☐ FALSE

Concepts 5: Texture, Structure and Design – General level

The texture, structure and design concepts you need to know about at General level are the same as those for Foundation level *plus*:

- duet
- improvisation
- rondo
- canon
- binary form (AB)
- ternary form (ABA, AABA)
- minuet and trio
- chord
- arpeggio
- note cluster
- organum
- walking bass

- descant
- fanfare
- concerto
- symphony
- slow air
- Gaelic psalms (long tunes)
- Scots ballad
- bothy ballad
- pibroch
- waulking song
- mouth music (port a beul).

Ten-Minute Tester

Jot down what you already know about each of the texture, structure and design concepts listed above. If you are unsure about any of the concepts revise them thoroughly before attempting Listening Exercise 23.

Listening Exercise 23: CD track 23

Read the questions below very carefully before listening to CD track 23. Try to answer the questions after hearing the recorded excerpt no more than **twice** (once for each question).

Question 1. Listen to CD track 23 and identify the vocal style. Tick **one** box.

- ☐ Mouth music
- ☐ Gaelic psalm
- ☐ Waulking song
- ☐ Organum

HOW TO PASS STANDARD GRADE MUSIC

Question 2. Listen to CD track 23 again and identify a feature present. Tick **one** box.

☐ Walking bass

☐ Descant

☐ Arpeggio

☐ Improvisation

Concepts 5: Texture, Structure and Design – Credit level

The features of texture, structure and design you need to know about at Credit level are the same as those for both Foundation and General levels *plus*:

- tierce de Picardie
- word painting
- word setting
- tempo
- augmentation
- diminution
- pedal
- inverted pedal
- ground bass
- alberti bass
- homophonic
- polyphonic
- contrapuntal (counterpoint)
- obbligato
- counter-melody
- suspension
- passing note

- suite (related pieces)
- fugue
- sonata
- scherzo
- cantata
- oratorio
- chorale
- recitative
- aria
- chorus
- programme music
- strophic
- through-composed
- quartet
- coda
- cadenza
- serial.

Ten-Minute Tester

Jot down what you already know about each of the texture, structure and design concepts listed above. If you are unsure about any of the concepts revise them thoroughly before attempting Listening Exercises 24 and 25.

Listening Exercise 24: CD track 24

Read the questions below very carefully before listening to CD track 24. Try to answer the questions after hearing the recorded excerpt no more than **twice** (once for each question).

Question 1. Listen to CD track 24 and tick **two** boxes to describe the kind of singing you hear.

☐ Polyphonic

☐ Chorus

☐ Word painting

☐ Strophic

Question 2. Listen to CD track 24 again and tick **one** box to identify the type of composition.

☐ Scherzo

☐ Cantata

☐ Aria

☐ Chorale

Listening Exercise 25: CD track 25

Read the questions below very carefully before listening to CD track 25. Try to answer the questions after hearing the recorded excerpt no more than **twice** (once for each question).

Question 1. Listen to CD track 25 and tick **one** box to identify the type of composition.

☐ Fugue

☐ Sonata

☐ Quartet

☐ Serial

☐ Programme music

Question 2. Listen to CD track 25 again and identify a feature present. Tick **one** box.

☐ Pedal bass

☐ Counterpoint

☐ Tierce de Picardie

☐ Cadenza

☐ Alberti bass

HOW TO PASS STANDARD GRADE MUSIC

Concepts 6: Harmony – Foundation level

At Foundation level you should be able to:

◆ recognise when a chord changes in a piece of music.

For Practice

You should practise for the following exercise by listening carefully to some songs of your own choice and trying to identify where chord changes take place. You can listen to your favourite songs for this, but it's best to start with something simple – a song where the chords don't change too often – until you get used to identifying chord changes by ear.

Listening Exercise 26: CD track 26

Question 1. Below are the lyrics (words) to the song excerpt on CD track 26. Read them very carefully and then, as you listen to the excerpt, place a cross (**X**) above the words where a chord change takes place. The first two crosses have been inserted for you as an example. Try to complete this exercise after listening to the recorded excerpt no more than **three** times.

INTRODUCTION

       X   X
Shine on Ruby Mountain, from the valley to the sea.

Shine on Ruby Mountain, shine your sweet love down on me.

Concepts 6: Harmony – General level

The harmony concepts you need to know about at General level are the same as that for Foundation level *plus*:

◆ recognise specific chord changes in a piece of music where the chords are I, IV and V in major keys

◆ tonality (major and minor keys)

◆ simple blues/rock chord progression.

Ten-Minute Tester

Jot down what you already know about each of the harmony concepts listed on page 26. If you are unsure about any of the concepts revise them thoroughly before attempting Listening Exercise 27.

For Practice

You can practise for the following exercise by listening carefully to some simple songs (which use only chords I, IV and V) and trying to identify where a chord change takes place, and whether the chord is I, IV or V. Your teacher can advise you on choosing songs for this exercise.

Listening Exercise 27: CD track 27

Question 1. Below are the lyrics (words) to the song excerpt on CD track 27. Read them very carefully and then, as you listen to the excerpt, identify the chord being played at those points where a box appears (the key is E♭ major). The chords you are asked to identify are: **E♭** (Chord I), **A♭** (Chord IV) and **B♭** (Chord V). You should write either the chord name or number only in the boxes provided. The first chord has been inserted for you as an example. Try to complete this question after listening to the recorded excerpt no more than **three** times.

INTRODUCTION

I
E♭

Goin' back to Kansas City, Kansas City here I come.

☐ ☐

Goin' back to Kansas City, Kansas City here I come, yeah

☐ ☐ ☐

I'm gonna find my baby and we're gonna have some fun.

Question 2. Listen to CD track 27 again and decide whether the tonality (key) is MAJOR or MINOR. Tick **one** box.

☐ The tonality is MAJOR

☐ The tonality is MINOR

Concepts 6: Harmony – Credit level

The harmony concepts you need to know about at Credit level are the same as those for both Foundation and General levels *plus*:

◆ recognise specific chord changes in a piece of music where the chords are I, IV, V and VI in major and minor keys

◆ recognise perfect and imperfect cadences

◆ discord/dissonance

◆ recognise when a piece of music modulates (changes) to another key.

Ten-Minute Tester

Jot down what you already know about each of the harmony concepts listed above. If you are unsure about any of the concepts revise them thoroughly before attempting Listening Exercise 28.

For Practice

You can practise for the following exercise by listening carefully to some songs where only chords I, IV, V and VI are used and trying to identify which of these is playing whenever a chord change takes place. Your teacher can advise you on choosing songs for this exercise.

Listening Exercise 28: CD track 28

Question 1. The lyrics (words) to the song excerpt on CD track 28 are on the following page. Read them very carefully and then, as you listen to the excerpt, identify the chord being played at those points where a box appears (the key is A major). The chords you are asked to identify are: **A** (Chord I), **D** (Chord IV), **E** (Chord V) and **F♯ minor** (Chord VI). You should write either the chord name or number only in the boxes provided. The first chord has been inserted for you as an example. Try to complete this question after listening to the recorded excerpt no more than **three** times.

I
A

☐

Everybody's looking for that something, one thing that makes it all complete.

☐   ☐

You find it in the strangest places, places you never knew it could be.

☐   ☐

Some find it in the face of their children, some find it in their lover's eyes

☐   ☐

Who can deny the joy it brings, you've found that special thing,

☐

You're flying without wings.

Question 2. Listen to CD track 28 again and tick **one** box to describe the cadence you hear at the end of the **second** line (above). Try to complete this question after listening to the recorded excerpt again no more than **twice**.

☐ Perfect cadence

☐ Imperfect cadence

Concepts 7: Dynamics – Foundation level

At Foundation level you should know about:

- **pp** (pianissimo)
- **p** (piano)
- **mp** (mezzo piano)
- **mf** (mezzo forte)

- **f** (forte)
- **ff** (fortissimo)
- crescendo (*cresc.*)
- diminuendo (*dim.*).

Ten-Minute Tester

If you are unsure about any of the above dynamics concepts revise them thoroughly before moving on to the listening exercise which follows.

Listening Exercise 29: CD track 29

Read the questions below very carefully before listening to CD track 29. Try to answer the questions after listening to the recorded excerpt no more than **twice** (once for each question).

Question 1. Listen to CD track 29 and tick the box which best describes the dynamic of the music just before the **end** of this excerpt. Tick **one** box.

☐ *pp* (pianissimo)

☐ *mp* (mezzo piano)

☐ *mf* (mezzo forte)

☐ *ff* (fortissimo)

Question 2. Listen to CD track 29 again and tick **one** box to identify another feature present.

☐ Crescendo

☐ Diminuendo

Concepts 7: Dynamics – General level

The dynamics concepts you need to know about at General level are the same as those for Foundation level *plus*:

◆ methods of changing dynamic gradation (e.g. adding or subtracting instruments in a piece of music).

There are no listening exercises in this section, but you should be aware that the volume levels (dynamics) in a piece of music will be altered not only when the musicians play their instruments louder or quieter, but also when the number of musicians playing at any one time is reduced. To hear this technique in practice, work through the following exercise.

For Practice

Choose a fairly large piece of music for orchestra, such as a symphony or a concerto, and listen carefully to how the instruments of the orchestra are used. Not every instrument will play during the entire piece; there will be times when perhaps just the strings or woodwind are playing, or the brass and percussion. When this happens, does the dynamic level alter? Without the full orchestra playing, does the music become quieter? What happens to the dynamic level when the full orchestra play together? As you listen, notice how the composer can constantly alter the dynamics in the piece not only through changes in volume but also by varying the number of musicians playing at any one time.

Concepts 7: Dynamics – Credit level

The dynamics concepts you need to know about at Credit level are the same as those for both Foundation and General level.

More practice with musical concepts

For Practice

For further practice with all of the musical concepts you have just revised, you can repeat the previous exercises by referring to the questions/concepts again as you listen to different kinds of music. Also, try listening out for the concepts each time you listen to your favourite music.

Buddy Study

Using the exercises in this chapter as a guide, why not make up listening tests for each other by choosing your own musical excerpts and then setting questions on these for others in the group to tackle?

LISTENING

During your Standard Grade Music course you will practise identifying various musical features (or concepts) by listening to different kinds of music. You will also get some experience responding to past Listening test papers where you answer questions on recorded musical excerpts.

The final Listening tests are assessed at Foundation, General and Credit levels, each one lasting for a different period of time:

◆ Foundation Listening test: approximately 45 minutes
◆ Foundation and General Listening test: approximately 1 hour 30 minutes
◆ General and Credit Listening test: approximately 1 hour 45 minutes.

The following sample Listening test papers present you with the types of questions you can expect at each level, and you will respond to those questions after listening to recorded excerpts on the CD which accompanies this book. (Answers are given at the back of the book.)

Note: your final Listening test will contain a few more questions than are presented in the following test papers, but the *types* of questions will be the same.

Preparing for the Listening test

One of the best ways to prepare for your Standard Grade Listening test is to listen to different kinds of music on a regular basis. This will keep your ear 'trained' in identifying the features in pieces of music.

It is also enjoyable to listen for and identify these features with a group of fellow students and compare your observations. By doing this you will help each other and become better at picking out all the important musical elements.

Ways of accessing different kinds of music

You might be able to hear, borrow or obtain lots of different types of music through the following sources:

◆ music teachers
◆ friends
◆ family members
◆ friends' parents

◆ radio
◆ local library
◆ the Internet
◆ music promotions in shops

Sample Listening test paper – Foundation level

Section I

Write your answers to the following questions (in pencil) in the spaces provided. Unless otherwise stated, you should try to answer each question after listening to each track **once**.

Question 1

CD track 30. Listen to CD track 30 and from the list below identify the group of instruments you hear playing in this excerpt.

Choose from:

A FOLK GROUP

A POP GROUP

A ROCK GROUP

A JAZZ GROUP

A SCOTTISH DANCE BAND

This piece is played by _____

Question 2

CD track 31. Listen to CD track 31 and tick the best description of what you hear.

☐ Voices

☐ Voices and instruments

☐ Instruments

Question 3

CD track 32. Listen to CD track 32 and decide if there is an OSTINATO present. Tick **one** box.

The piece has an OSTINATO. ☐ TRUE **or** ☐ FALSE

Question 4

CD track 33. Listen to CD track 33 and decide if the melody moves mainly by STEP or mainly by LEAP. Tick **one** box.

The melody moves mainly by STEP ☐ **or** mainly by LEAP ☐

Question 5

CD track 34. Listen to CD track 34 and decide if there are THREE beats or FOUR beats in the bar. Tick **one** box.

There are THREE beats in the bar ☐ **or** there are FOUR beats in the bar ☐

Listen to CD track 34 again and decide if repetition is present. Tick **one** box.

Repetition is present. ☐ TRUE **or** ☐ FALSE

Question 6

CD track 35. Listen to CD track 35 and tick **one** box from COLUMN A and **one** box from COLUMN B to describe what you hear. You can listen to the excerpt **twice**.

Tick **one** box in each column.

COLUMN A

☐ Bowing
☐ Plucking
☐ Blowing

COLUMN B

☐ Solo
☐ Ensemble

Question 7

CD track 36. Listen to the accompaniment (or backing) in the song on CD track 36 and identify where the chord (or harmony) changes.

Put a cross (**X**) either **above** each word where a change takes place, or, if you hear a chord change taking place just **before** a word is sung, put a cross (**X**) **before** that word. The first **four** changes have been inserted for you (notice that there are two places where a chord change occurs before a word). You can listen to the excerpt up to **three** times.

                    X
As morning breaks, the heaven on high

X   **X**
I lift my heavy load to the skies

X

Sun come down with a burning glow

Mingles my sweat with the earth below

Oh island in the sun

Willed to me by my father's hand

All my days I will sing in praise

Of your forest water, your shining sun.

Section II

Question 8

CD track 37. Listen to CD track 37 and describe the style of music you hear by selecting from the list below.

Choose from:

FOLK

POP

SWING

ROCK 'N' ROLL

RAGTIME

This is an example of _____

Question 9

CD track 38. Listen to CD track 38 and select the correct description of SCOTTISH music you hear from the selection below.

Choose from:

MARCH

JIG

STRATHSPEY

WALTZ

This is an example of a _____

Listen to CD track 38 again and decide if a LEAD-IN is present. Tick **one** box.

A lead-in is present. ☐ TRUE **or** ☐ FALSE

Question 10

CD track 39. Listen to CD track 39 and tick **one** box from COLUMN A and **one** box from COLUMN B to describe what you hear. You can listen to the excerpt **twice**.

Tick **one** box in each column.

COLUMN A	COLUMN B
☐ Solo voice	☐ Accompanied
☐ Voices in unison/octaves	☐ Unaccompanied
☐ Voices in harmony	

Question 11

CD track 40. Listen to CD track 40 and decide if there is a SEQUENCE present. Tick **one** box.

A SEQUENCE is present. ☐ TRUE **or** ☐ FALSE

Question 12

CD track 41. Listen to CD track 41 and decide which family of instruments from the orchestra is playing.

Choose from:

WOODWIND

BRASS

PERCUSSION

STRINGS

The music is played by the _____

Sample Listening test paper – General level

Section I

Write your answers to the following questions (in pencil) in the spaces provided.

Question 1

CD track 42. Listen to CD track 42 and identify the type of group playing. Tick **one** box.

☐ Brass band

☐ Gamelan

☐ Steel band

☐ Pipe band

☐ Orchestra

Question 2

This question is based on electric/electronic music.

(a)

CD track 43. Listen to CD track 43 and identify **two** features present. Tick **two** boxes.

☐ Sequence

☐ Ostinato

☐ Electric guitar

☐ Electric drums

☐ Walking bass

(b)

CD track 44. Listen to CD track 44 and tick **one** box in COLUMN A to identify the solo instrument and **one** box in COLUMN B to identify the style of playing.

Tick **one** box in each column.

COLUMN A	COLUMN B
☐ Synthesiser	☐ Staccato melody
☐ Electric guitar	☐ Legato melody
☐ Bass guitar	

(c)

Listen to CD track 44 again and identify **two** features present. Tick **two** boxes.

☐ Repetition

☐ Riff

☐ Note clusters

☐ Arpeggios

(d)

CD track 45. Listen to CD track 45 and tick **two** boxes to identify the musical features present.

☐ Electric guitar

☐ Rubato

☐ Accelerando

☐ Sforzando

☐ Synthesiser

(e)

CD track 46. Listen to CD track 46 and tick the correct description of what you hear. Tick **one** box.

☐ Ornaments

☐ Arpeggios

☐ Rallentando

☐ Scotch snap

☐ Grace note

Question 3

This question features Scottish music.

(a)

CD track 47. Listen to CD track 47 and tick **one** box to describe what you hear.

☐ Waltz

☐ Reel

☐ Jig

☐ Strathspey

(b)

CD track 48. Listen to CD track 48 and identify the vocal style. Tick **one** box.

☐ Gaelic psalm

☐ Bothy ballad

☐ Mouth music

☐ Waulking song

Question 4

This question features orchestral music.

(a)

CD track 49. Listen to CD track 49 and identify the **solo** instrument. Tick **one** box.

☐ Flute

☐ Violin

☐ Cello

☐ Double bass

(b)

CD track 50. Listen to CD track 50 and tick **two** boxes to describe what you hear.

☐ Rondo

☐ Sequence

☐ Crescendo

☐ Sforzando

(c)

CD track 51. Listen to CD track 51 and identify two features present. Tick **two** boxes.

☐ Accelerando

☐ Pizzicato

☐ Imitation

☐ Syncopation

Question 5

This question is about chord changes. The song is in the key of **C** major.

The chords you are asked to identify are:

C   Chord I

F   Chord IV

G   Chord V

CD track 52. Listen to CD track 52 and write **either** the chord name **or** number only in the boxes provided. The first two chords have been inserted for you as an example. Try to complete this question after listening to the recorded excerpt no more than **three** times.

INTRODUCTION

I		IV			
C		F		☐	☐

Someday I'm gonna write the story of my life;

☐   ☐   ☐   ☐

I'll tell about the night we met and how my heart can't forget

☐   ☐   ☐   ☐

The way you smiled   at me.

Section II

Question 6

(a)

CD track 53. Listen to CD track 53 and identify the musical style. Tick **one** box.

- ☐ Blues
- ☐ Swing
- ☐ Ragtime
- ☐ Folk
- ☐ Salsa

(b)

Listen to CD track 53 again and tick **one** box to identify a feature present.

- ☐ Round
- ☐ Sforzando
- ☐ Four beats in a bar
- ☐ Accelerando

Question 7

(a)

CD track 54. Listen to CD track 54 and identify the type of voice you hear. Tick **one** box.

- ☐ Soprano
- ☐ Alto
- ☐ Tenor
- ☐ Bass

(b)

CD track 55. Listen to CD track 55 and tick **one** box to identify the instrument playing the melody.

- ☐ Clarinet
- ☐ Trumpet
- ☐ Saxophone
- ☐ Trombone

(c)

Listen to track 55 again and tick **one** box to identify a feature present.

- ☐ Crescendo
- ☐ Canon
- ☐ Vamp
- ☐ Three beats in a bar

Question 8

(a)

CD track 56. Listen to CD track 56 and tick **one** box to describe what you hear.

- ☐ Ghanaian drum ensemble
- ☐ Electronic drums
- ☐ Gamelan
- ☐ Latin percussion ensemble

(b)

Listen to track 56 again and tick **two** boxes to describe what you hear.

- ☐ Imitation
- ☐ Flute
- ☐ Drone
- ☐ Improvisation

(c)

CD track 57. Listen to CD track 57 and tick the correct description of what you hear. Tick **one** box.

- ☐ Major key
- ☐ Minor key
- ☐ Syncopation
- ☐ Riff

(d)

Listen to CD track 57 again and tick **two** boxes to describe what you hear.

- ☐ Walking bass
- ☐ Accelerando
- ☐ Improvisation
- ☐ Organ
- ☐ Slow air

Question 9

In this question you will be asked to identify musical styles/forms.

(a)

CD track 58. Listen to CD track 58 and tick **one** box to identify the style/form.

☐ Musical

☐ Concerto

☐ Baroque

☐ Symphony

☐ Opera

(b)

CD track 59. Listen to CD track 59 and tick **one** box to identify the style/form.

☐ Musical

☐ Concerto

☐ Baroque

☐ Symphony

☐ Opera

(c)

CD track 60. Listen to CD track 60 and tick **one** box to identify the style/form.

☐ Musical

☐ Concerto

☐ Baroque

☐ Symphony

☐ Opera

 Sample Listening test paper – Credit level

Section I

Write your answers to the following questions (in pencil) in the spaces provided.

Question 1. This question is about vocal music.

(a)

CD track 61. Listen to CD track 61 and identify the style of the piece. Tick **one** box.

☐ Baroque

☐ Classical

☐ Romantic

☐ Impressionist

(b)

Listen to CD track 61 again and tick **three** boxes to identify features of this excerpt.

☐ Recitative

☐ Melismatic

☐ Imitation

☐ Aria

☐ Homophony

☐ Polyphony

☐ A capella

(c)

CD track 62. Listen to CD track 62 and tick **one** box to identify a feature of the bass in this excerpt.

☐ Pedal

☐ Pizzicato

☐ Alberti bass

☐ Obbligato

(d)

CD track 63. Listen to CD track 63 and tick **one** box in COLUMN A to describe the style of the music and **one** box in COLUMN B to identify a feature of the accompaniment.

Tick **one** box in each column.

COLUMN A	COLUMN B
☐ Negro spiritual	☐ Syncopation
☐ Ragtime	☐ Pedal
☐ Reggae	☐ Contrary motion
☐ Swing	☐ Alberti bass

Question 2.

(a)

CD track 64. Listen to CD track 64 and tick **two** boxes to identify features of this excerpt.

☐ Rubato

☐ Folk

☐ Bothy ballad

☐ Three beats per bar

(b)

Listen to CD track 64 again and tick **one** box to identify a feature in the **accompaniment**.

☐ Contrary motion

☐ Ostinato

☐ Inverted pedal

☐ Arpeggios

Question 3. This question is about chord changes.

The song is in the key of G major, and the chords used are:

G   Chord I

C   Chord IV

D   Chord V

Em   Chord VI

CD track 65. Listen to CD track 65 and complete the blank boxes, using the chords shown above. You can write **either** the chord name **or** number in the boxes. The first chord has been inserted for you. You can listen to the excerpt up to **three** times.

I
G

☐   ☐

...I'm loving angels instead.   And through it all she offers me protection

☐   ☐

A lot of love and affection, whether I'm right or wrong.

☐ ☐

And down the waterfall   wherever it may take me,

☐ ☐

I know that life won't break   me when I come to call …

Question 4. In this question you will listen to a musical excerpt which is about the QE2, the famous luxury cruise ship, and then describe how the composer uses musical means to suggest:

1   **The ship's powerful propellers disturbing the water's surface**

2   **A change in the ship's speed which might suggest that it has left harbour and entered the open sea**

3   **The ship's foghorn/siren**

4   **Water breaking over the ship's bow as it cuts through the waves**

You should refer to at least **three** of the following:

Rhythm/tempo   Melody/harmony   Orchestration   Dynamics

You might wish to make rough notes as you listen, then write your final answers in the boxes below. You can listen to the excerpt up to **three** times.

CD track 66. Listen to CD track 66 and note your final answers in the table provided.

Final answers

Musical Aspect	Musical means and effect created
Rhythm/tempo	
Melody/harmony	
Orchestration	
Dynamics	

Section II

Question 5. This question features ballet music.

(a)

CD track 67. Listen to CD track 67 and focus on the **string** parts. Tick **two** boxes to identify features present.

☐ Pedal

☐ Arpeggios

☐ Pizzicato

☐ Alberti bass

(b)

Listen to CD track 67 again and this time focus on the **woodwind** parts. Tick **two** boxes to identify features present.

☐ Pizzicato

☐ Inverted pedal

☐ Sequence

☐ Trill

☐ Imitation

(c)

Listen to CD track 67 one more time and identify the scale played by the flute in this excerpt. You can listen for the scale up to **two** times.

☐ Major

☐ Minor

☐ Whole-tone

☐ Pentatonic

(d)

CD track 68. Listen to CD track 68 and tick **one** box in COLUMN A to identify the key of the music, **one** box in COLUMN B to identify a feature of the orchestral accompaniment, and **one** box in COLUMN C to identify the solo instrument.

Tick **one** box in each column.

COLUMN A	COLUMN B	COLUMN C
☐ Major	☐ Ground bass	☐ Flute
☐ Minor	☐ Syncopation	☐ Oboe
☐ Atonal	☐ Tremolo	☐ Bassoon

(e)

Listen to CD track 68 again and identify the cadence at the end of the excerpt. You can listen for the cadence up to **two** times.

The cadence at the end of the excerpt is _____

Question 6. In this question you will listen to two contrasting versions of the same piece. As you listen, comment on the **instruments** and how they are used, on the **rhythm/tempo** and on the **tonality** in each version.

You might wish to make rough notes as you listen, then write your final answers in the boxes below. You can listen to each excerpt up to **two** times.

CD tracks 69 and 70. Listen carefully to CD track 69 and compare it with CD track 70. Note your final answers in the table provided.

Final answers

	Version one	Version two
Instruments and how they are used		
Rhythm/tempo		
Tonality		

Question 7. This question features music for piano.

(a)

CD track 71. Listen to CD track 71 and tick **two** boxes to identify features present.

☐ Cross rhythms

☐ Rubato

☐ Inverted pedal

☐ Clusters

(b)

CD track 72. Listen to CD track 72 and tick **two** boxes to identify features present.

☐ Inverted pedal

☐ Impressionism

☐ Rubato

☐ Cross rhythms

(c)

CD track 73. Listen to CD track 73 and tick **two** boxes to identify features present.

☐ Arpeggios

☐ Clusters

☐ Contrary motion

☐ Diminuendo

Question 8. This question is based on the song 'Ruby (Don't Take Your Love To Town)'.

Listed below are six features which occur in the music. Above the appropriate point in the text, you should indicate where each feature occurs. **You should write the number of each feature once only and in the boxes provided.**

Give yourself about one minute to read through the features, and listen to the excerpt up to **three** times.

1 **Backing vocals**

2 **First entry of acoustic guitar playing a sequence**

3 **Pause**

4 **Second entry of acoustic guitar playing a sequence**

5 **Acoustic guitar enters**

6 **Acoustic guitar repeats sequence at a higher pitch**

CD track 74. Listen to CD track 74 and respond to the following exercise in the manner described on page 50.

INTRODUCTION

☐

You've painted up your lips and rolled and curled your tinted hair

Ruby are you contemplating going out somewhere

The shadow on the wall tells me the sun is going down

☐   ☐   ☐

Oh Ruby   don't take your love to town.

☐

It wasn't me that started that old crazy Asian war

☐

But I was proud to go and do my patriotic chore.

Extra Listening Practice

Buddy Study

Select a few recordings of different types of music, such as classical, pop, Scottish and jazz, and choose a section from each. Play each section at least twice and, using a chart like the one below, write down your observations as you listen. You will probably hear more new things each time you listen. At the end of the exercise, compare notes with your buddies.

Buddy Study continued ➤

Buddy Study continued

Listening observation chart

Piece	Style	Features
Beethoven's Fifth Symphony (first movement)	classical	orchestra rhythmic motif crescendos rhythmic ostinato repetition key changes counterpoint **ff**

Buddy Study

Why not set Listening tests for each other? You can take turns at selecting a piece of music and preparing questions on it for the other group members, based upon the features you can identify in it. As a guide for this exercise, you might use questions from the sample Listening tests in this book, or just make up your own. Another option is to have your buddies 're-sit' the sample Listening test papers, but *you* select different musical excerpts to 'fit' with the sample answers.

INVENTING

Throughout your Standard Grade Music course you will build up a selection of your own musical inventions, the best of which will be recorded and assessed by your teacher (this work will count towards your final grade).

The three main Inventing activities you will experience are **Composing**, **Improvising** and **Arranging**.

In this section we will cover these three activities through a series of workshops and Inventing exercises which put into practice many of the musical concepts you will have learned on the course. You can use these exercises to revise things you already know, or to help you invent new pieces. The material will also be a good source of reference for the future if you are going on to study music beyond Standard Grade.

Finding inspiration

Getting ideas for composing a piece of music isn't difficult. Just observing things while out walking can provide some inspiration: the group of magpies bouncing across a lawn; trees nodding and swaying in a gale; a lone seagull gliding effortlessly in a cloudless sky; the bustle of cars, buses and people on the street; the loneliness in the eyes of a homeless person on the street corner. Listening to different kinds of music is another great way to get some inspiration – as well as hearing how experienced composers get their ideas across.

Over the centuries, people have written music about people, places and human feelings (think about how many pop songs are about people and human relationships). Here are some things that could inspire you to compose a piece of music:

◆ **your feelings about something or someone** – a love song; an angry piece of rock music; an instrumental piece (one without words) whose *mood* describes your inner feelings

◆ **a place** – a beautiful Scottish island; the turbulent surface of Saturn; a mythical fairy glen

◆ **an event** – the Olympic Games; Christmas; an air show; a Formula One race

◆ **humour** – the state of your bedroom; your crazy pet dog; the short-sighted wizard who keeps getting his potions wrong because he misreads his magic recipe book

- **the supernatural** – ghosts; witches; vampires; the spooky atmosphere in the old, ruined castle
- **nature** – a violent thunderstorm; gentle summer rain; the seaside
- **improvising** – playing around with different chords and scales often triggers ideas.

But a piece of music doesn't have to be about anything in particular; you may just like how certain notes and chords sound together and build a piece that way. The finished work could be called something like 'Study', or you might simply use the musical tempo of the piece (*andante*, *allegro*, *lento*, etc.) for your title, just as many famous composers did. It doesn't matter as long as the finished product is musical and you are happy with it.

Buddy Study

Get together with some of your fellow students and make a list of all the different things you could write a piece of music about. When you have made your list, discuss how these ideas might be expressed in music. What would be the mood of each piece? How would you create that mood? Which scales/keys would you choose? Which musical techniques? Which instruments would be most effective for the various styles of the pieces?

Putting your ideas to music

When you speak, the words you choose and the tone of your voice will help to express what you are talking about. If you are describing your personal experience of a terrifying roller-coaster ride, your voice will sound different to those times when you complain about how much homework you've just been given for the weekend. The excitement in your voice as you recall the hair-raising drops, twists and sharp turns of the roller-coaster ride will better *describe* the experience to others (only *you* can create a clear picture in their minds' eyes), just as your low, sad voice will describe equally well how you feel about the load of homework – and if you do that well enough, others might feel sorry for you too (although it's unlikely your teacher will!).

When you are inventing music you have to do the same thing, except that words become notes (or song lyrics) and musical **rhythm**, and the **key, tempo,** and **dynamics** of the piece will be your tone of voice – all expressed by the musical instruments you choose. Think of your invention then as a kind of story; it will have a beginning, middle and end, and it has to be interesting or people will get bored.

Let's consider how the notes in different **scales** might help create certain moods and feelings:

- **major scale** – happy; pleasant
- **minor scale** – sad or serious
- **chromatic scale** – several possibilities: can be humorous or serious; can also give a strong impression of upward movement (when played **ascending**) or downward movement (when played **descending** – something to think about if you are writing a piece about flying, or a rocket launch!)
- **pentatonic scale** – a versatile scale used in blues, rock, jazz and Scottish music; popular for **improvising**
- **blues scale** – used only in blues music
- **whole-tone scale** – calm; peaceful; dreamy; can give the impression of open spaces or soaring high above the clouds
- **atonal scale** – serious; scary; supernatural; good for creating a haunting mood.

Buddy Study

Get together in a group and play each of the scales listed above (refer to the section on melody in the glossary of musical concepts, if you need to) then discuss whether you all think they express the moods and ideas suggested. Discuss what other ideas come to mind and make a note of these. Remember, experimenting like this is often how composers come to write their best music.

Once you have decided on the kind of piece you are going to write, and the scale (or scales) that are likely to suit your idea, you will then be ready to start composing.

Inventing Workshop 1: Composing a Song

Building vocal phrases

We all speak in **phrases**; short units of speech that have **rhythm**, **pitch** and little **pauses** as we breathe and express each word. Lots of phrases make up bigger conversations, just as musical phrases build larger compositions.

Consider the following sentence or phrase:

From the dungeon came the cry, 'let me go or let me die.'

Try saying this phrase out loud, just as though you were speaking *naturally* to someone sitting opposite, and listen carefully to the sound of your voice. Notice how the words have their own natural **rhythm**. Did the **pitch** of your voice alter slightly as you spoke? Did it fall towards the end of the phrase? Did you pause a little after the word *cry*?

This phrase fits naturally into two parts; the first part ends with the natural pause created by the comma after the word '*cry*', and the second part begins on the word '*let*' and closes with the full stop. In music, these two parts would form a **Question-and-Answer** statement.

├─   Question statement   ─┤ ├─Answer statement─┤

From the dungeon came the cry,   'let me go or let me die.'

Adding musical rhythm

Now we can concentrate on transferring the natural rhythm of the words into musical rhythm. The easiest way to begin doing this is to add a musical note to every *syllable* of the phrase.

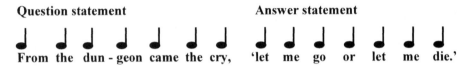

Question statement   **Answer statement**

From the dun - geon came the cry,   'let   me   go   or   let   me   die.'

If we left it like this it would be pretty monotonous since the note values are all the same length – in this case a crotchet or quarter note. To make the rhythm more interesting therefore we need to vary the note values whilst still keeping some of the natural rhythm of the words. When doing this, it is helpful to remember that wherever there is a pause in the natural rhythm of a phrase (for example, where there is a comma, full stop, colon or semicolon), this is normally a good place to put either a **rest** or a note of longer value.

Q   **A**

From the dun - geon came the   cry,   'let   me   go   or   let   me   die.'

Of course this is just one of several possible rhythms we could have chosen. Another might have been:

Q   **A**

From   the   dun - geon came the cry,   'let   me   go   or   let   me   die.'

Adding a time signature

As we speak we put more emphasis on some words and syllables than others. Which words and syllables of our phrase would you naturally put more emphasis on? Say the phrase out loud again slowly to work this out, then put an **accent** above each word or syllable which is emphasised.

Here is my version:

Q   **A**

\>   \>   \>   \>   \>   \>   \>   \>

From the dun – geon came the cry,   **'let me go or let me die.'**

This naturally occurring emphasis is very useful when it comes to determining where the main beats are – which will help us decide how many beats we should have in a bar, and therefore what our **time signature** will be.

In the above example there are four **accents** in the Question statement, and four in the Answer, so we could have two bars of music with four beats in each bar. In this case, the second rhythm example above would fit well into a two-bar structure.

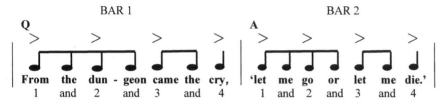

However, a more common structure is to have a two-bar Question statement followed by a two-bar Answer statement, giving one larger four-bar phrase. If we choose this option then the first rhythm example above would fit the four-bar structure.

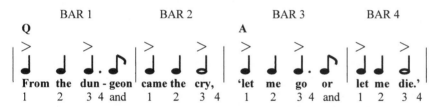

As well as playing around with the rhythm, you could also experiment with **anacrusis,** which would move the first beat of bar 1 onto a different word/syllable.

Hints and Tips

Phrases don't have to be two or four bars long of course; they can be any length, depending on the style of the music and the composer's interpretation. The phrase lengths in a piece of instrumental music, for instance, can vary a lot – but remember that without some phrase structure your music could sound as though it's just rambling on like someone with the most boring voice in the world!

Hitting the right note

With your time signature and rhythm worked out, all you need to do is choose notes which suit the mood of the words and your musical phrase will be complete.

When writing vocal music it is essential that the notes used can be sung comfortably (not too high or too low) so, if in doubt, play your intended notes on a keyboard and try singing them yourself.

The words in our phrase are not pleasant! So a minor scale/key would be a good choice – but you could try experimenting with the different sounds of other scales.

If we use the scale/key of **D Minor** our notes will be **D E F G A B♭ C♯**, but of course we can also use some of the **chromatic** notes in between if we wish.

Once again there are guidelines that can help us to choose effective notes for a phrase. The phrase can begin on any note (although using the key note here will help to establish the key), but if we want to emphasise the effect that it has ended (on the word '*die*') then a **perfect cadence** would work well as this produces a 'full-stop' effect. So, the second-to-last note in our phrase needs to be found in either the chord of G minor (chord IV) or A major (chord V), followed by the keynote, D (chord I) – see the section on common keys and their chords on pages 94–98. The example below begins on the key note, D, and uses C♯ (from chord V) and D (from chord I) to form the perfect cadence at the end.

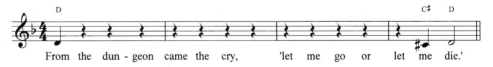

From the dun - geon came the cry, 'let me go or let me die.'

If we had preferred not to create the 'full-stop' effect at the end of the phrase, we could have used notes which are found in an **imperfect cadence**. An imperfect cadence makes us aware that more music is to follow, and can be made by simply reversing the order of a perfect cadence (for example, chord I followed by chord IV, or chord I followed by chord V).

Hints and Tips

The use of cadences will alter to suit different moods and phrase structures. For example, several phrases might end with an imperfect cadence before a perfect cadence is used.

It doesn't matter that we have begun by adding notes to the beginning and end of our phrase since getting these important landmarks right first will ensure we have a strong structure – and can even help us choose the remaining notes.

The Question-and-Answer structure of our four-bar phrase seems to be hinting at an **ascending** melody for the first two bars (the Question) followed by a two-bar **descending** melody (the Answer), just as our voices might naturally rise and fall when we say the phrase out loud. But there are no rules, and you should always be prepared to experiment with your own ideas.

Below is my own note choice for the full phrase, using my first rhythm example. Notice that I have used an A note on the word 'cry' (the end of the Question statement); this suggests chord V (A major), a good choice for the middle of a phrase where more music is to follow.

Hints and Tips

The phrase we have been working on here is an example of **syllabic** writing, but you could create even more rhythmic variety by including some **melismatic** writing.

For Practice

Select a few single sentences or phrases that you find interesting and set each of them to music, working through the process of adding rhythm, time signature, key, cadences and notes as outlined above. You can choose your sentences from books, poetry, or even a newspaper, or you can write your own, but make sure they fit comfortably into a Question-and-Answer structure in order to make your task easier. Pay particular attention also to choosing a key which suits the mood of each of your phrases, and notes that can be sung comfortably.

When writing a complete song, you can repeat the above process for each phrase of text and then play or sing it all back to check that everything fits well together, making any adjustments you like. Some phrases might be longer or shorter than others, but the method for setting them to music is the same as that outlined for the four-bar phrase.

Of course, this is not the only way to compose vocal music. For example, you might prefer to play around on the keyboard until the right notes and rhythm 'hit' you, or perhaps you already have ideas that just need to be expanded and written down or recorded. It doesn't matter, but you can always use the above composing methods if you get stuck for ideas at any stage.

Adding accompaniment to a melody

Whatever kind of piece you are composing, in most cases you will need to harmonise it by adding some kind of **accompaniment**. Accompaniments normally involve the use or understanding of chords, whether you decide to use simple chords in their traditional form (where each note of the chord is played at the same time) or opt for **arpeggios**, a **descant**, or a more complex **counter-melody**.

Let's look at some of the different ways in which we might harmonise our four-bar 'dungeon' phrase.

We can begin by choosing a chord to accompany each bar of the melody. The key is **D minor** so our basic chord choices are **D minor** (chord I), **G minor** (chord IV), **A major** (chord V) and **B♭ major** (chord VI). We could also add **F major**, from the **relative major** key. See the section on common keys and their chords on pages 94–98 for a review of all these chords.

For Practice

From the list above, choose a chord to accompany each bar of the dungeon phrase. You needn't use all of the chords, therefore the same chord can be used more than once. If you are a little more experienced, you might like to add more than one chord per bar, where possible; perhaps having a chord on beat 1 and another on beat 2, 3 or 4. You may also want to experiment with chord **inversions**, where the lowest note (the root note) of a chord is swapped for one of the other notes in that chord. For example:

For Practice continued ➢

D minor chord with **D**
as the lowest note
(**D**, F, A): the 'root
position' chord

D minor chord with **F**
as the lowest note
(**F**, A, D): the 'first
inversion' chord

D minor chord with **A**
as the lowest note
(**A**, D, F): the 'second
inversion' chord

To do this exercise, you can record the dungeon phrase using a keyboard or a computer and play it back while you experiment with the sounds of different accompanying chords or chord inversions. Alternatively, you could try this as a 'Buddy Study' exercise, where a fellow student plays the phrase while you work out the chords.

Hints and Tips

When choosing chords to accompany a melody you can simply experiment with different chords until you find the one that 'fits', but remember that it is helpful if you look for a chord that has a note (or notes) in common with the melody notes of each bar. For example, if a bar has the notes D and F in it, then the chord of D minor would fit with these notes since D minor also contains D and F.

Accompaniment variations

When you have added chords to your melody you then might want to try experimenting with some interesting accompaniment variations based on those chords.

Let's say your basic chord progression looks like this:

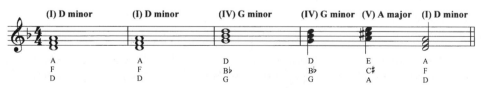

That will sound fine as it is, but you can also 'break up' the notes of each chord and play them successively, as arpeggios, to create different kinds of accompaniment textures. Here are a few possible accompaniment styles you could try:

Arpeggio pattern 1

D F A F D F A F   D F A F D F A F   G B♭ D B♭ G B♭ D B♭   G B♭ A C♯ D A D

Arpeggio pattern 2

D F A F D A D A   D F A F D A D A   G B♭ D B♭ G D G D   G B♭ A C♯ D A D

Alberti bass

D A F A D A F A   D A F A D A F A   G D B♭ D G D B♭ D   G D A C♯ D A D

Combination of arpeggio and basic chord

D F A F D   A   D F A F D   A   G B♭ D B♭ G   D   G B♭ A C♯ D   A
            F   F   B♭   F
            D   D   G   D

Here is an example of how the four-bar dungeon phrase might be accompanied by both chords *and* arpeggios (these two parts would be played on different musical instruments):

From the dun – geon | came the cry,   'let me go   or | let   me   die.'

D F A F D F A F   D F A F D F A F   G B♭ D B♭ G B♭ D B♭   G B♭ A C♯ D

Dminor   Dminor   Gminor   Gminor Amajor Dminor

Adding a bass part

When you have your accompaniment chords, adding a separate bass part is quite straightforward.

The simplest way to write a bass part is to take the *lowest* note of each chord you have chosen for the accompaniment and use it as a single bass note. For example:

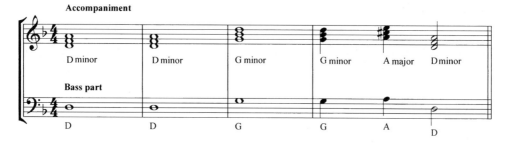

Notice that in the bass part each note has been dropped to sound an **octave** lower than the lowest notes of the accompaniment chords. By dropping the bass notes an octave (or even two octaves) you create a deep sound which adds to the texture of your composition.

Developing the bass part

To make our bass part even more interesting, we could try adding one or two additional notes to it (which 'fit' with everything else, of course) and give it a rhythm of its own. For example, the bass rhythm of the first bar of the phrase could be varied by having the note D on beat 1, then the note A (which is part of the D minor chord) on beat 4:

It wouldn't be a good idea to do this in every bar (unless of course you want this kind of repeating rhythm) as too much repetition can become boring, so you might choose to have two bass notes in bar 1, and just one bass note in bar 2.

When building up the bass part like this you just have to be careful not to make it too busy as it could interfere with the flow of the other parts, or make the music sound cluttered up with notes.

A simple but effective way to prevent the bass part interfering with a main melody is to use a less active bass part when the main melody is busy (has lots of notes) and use a busier bass part when the main melody is less active. For example:

In the last example both the bass part and the main melody use **passing notes**. These are very useful for building melodies – including more complex bass parts and counter-melodies – as you will see when you come to work on composing an instrumental piece in our next Inventing workshop.

CD Track 75. Below is my fully harmonised version of the four-bar dungeon phrase. You will see that I have developed the chord part using some chord **inversions**, and made the bass part a bit more active as well. You can hear the phrase on CD track 75 (note: the melody is not sung, but played on keyboard).

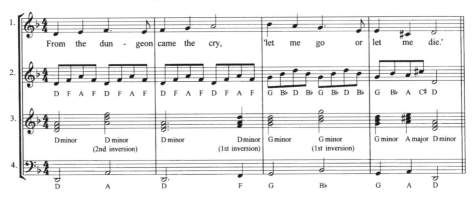

Each of the three accompaniment parts in the dungeon phrase has a different texture which could be performed on different kinds of instruments. For example, the arpeggios in part 2 might be played on a keyboard, piano, or guitar; part 3 would need a *harmonic* instrument (one capable of playing chords); and part 4 is intended for a bass instrument such as a double bass, cello, or bass guitar.

For Practice

Choose a complete short poem (no more than about sixteen lines in length) that has a fairly regular metre, and whose lines will fit comfortably into a **Question-and-Answer** structure, and try setting it to music, working through each of the processes of composition described in this workshop: beginning with the **rhythm** of the words, followed by note choice and **cadences**, gradually building up your piece by experimenting with various **chords**, **accompaniment styles** and a **bass part**.

Again, for a completely original touch you might choose to write your own words/lyrics as an alternative, but whether you do this or select a poem just make sure that the words give you enough opportunity for musical variety and expression – explosions, thunder, or stormy seas for instance!

For Practice continued ➤

For Practice *continued*

You can listen to each stage of your song's development as you compose it, either by playing it on a musical instrument or recording it using a keyboard or computer software. If you use a computer you can also experiment with the **timbre** by trying out different sounds and effects – this will be especially helpful when you want to hear the different accompaniment parts playing together. (But you could also do this with the help of some fellow musicians who could each play an accompaniment part on different instruments.)

Hints *and* **Tips**

Remember that most songs have two main elements: verses and chorus. The chorus is the catchy section which keeps returning in the song and which is normally sung to the same words each time, whereas the verses are sung to different words in between each repeat of the chorus. A closely related form to this is the **rondo**, where the 'A' section is repeated in between other contrasting sections of music. To get ideas for writing your own songs, listen carefully to different types of song and how they are structured.

Inventing Workshop 2: Composing an Instrumental Piece

We will now go through a step-by-step process of composing a lively piece of instrumental music with four parts, looking at how the musical concepts you have learned can help you do this, and how you can develop new material from just two simple bars of music – which is very useful if you ever get stuck for new ideas!

Developing a complete melody from just a few notes

While experimenting with the scale of A major one day, let's say you come up with two simple bars of music:

You like the idea but can't seem to invent anything effective to come after it. How can you build these two bars into a well-structured piece of music? Well, the good news is that there are lots of musical techniques (or 'little tricks') that you can use to develop even the simplest ideas whenever you get stuck.

65

This two-bar statement (the **Question**) needs another two-bar statement (an **Answer**) to balance it out. The Answer statement should be different yet still sound as though it's related to the Question statement.

A good technique to try out here would be **sequence**, where the same pattern of notes is repeated at either a higher or lower pitch. Let's try raising the Question statement up by four steps (a fourth).

The Answer statement is different but fits well with the Question statement to give us a nice four-bar phrase now.

The last note of the new four-bar phrase, D, creates the feeling that more music is to follow – this is because it isn't the key note, A. If we wanted the phrase to sound more complete we could change the note D for an A (to suggest a **perfect cadence**), but leaving things as they are keeps the momentum of the piece going here. And as this isn't vocal music our notes and phrase lengths don't have to follow the metre or rhythm of words.

Even though just four bars have been composed so far, it might be helpful to sketch out a rough plan for the whole piece at this stage as it will give us a visual reference of the intended overall structure. The plan doesn't have to be very precise at the start since we can alter it as our ideas develop.

Planning a structure early on will not only help us see where each musical feature should go, but also ensure that the finished product sounds balanced. Of course, not all music has a definite structure or form (if it doesn't, this is called **through-composed** music), but when you are experimenting with inventing it often helps if you stick to some kind of structure.

Musical form or structure

Structures we might choose for instrumental music include **theme and variations, minuet and trio, canon, binary form** and **rondo**, but one of the most popular and effective for short instrumental pieces is **ternary form**. This structure has three main sections (A, B, A), normally of equal length. You can consider this three-part structure as the beginning, middle and end of your piece, where the beginning sets out the first musical ideas, the middle has some **contrast**, and the end repeats the first musical ideas (possibly with some **variation**), and concludes the piece, perhaps using a **coda**.

A reasonable number of bars for each section is about eight, which will make our final piece twenty-four bars long (three times eight bars), but if we decide to repeat a section (or sections) this will extend our piece even more.

INVENTING

With that basic information, and our first four-bar phrase written, the plan of our piece could look like this:

'A' SECTION The 'Beginning' – first musical ideas

First ----	-- 4-bar ---	-- phrase -----------					

Bar: 1   2   3   4   5   6   7   8

'B' SECTION The 'Middle' – contrast

Bars 9–16 ---

'A' SECTION The 'End' – repeats first musical ideas

Repeat ---	-- of first ---	-- 4-bar -----	-- phrase				

Bars 17–24 --

Now that we can clearly see the overall planned structure of the entire composition, we can continue piecing it all together.

In order to complete the A section, we need to write a second four-bar phrase that will sound as though it's a natural continuation of the first.

To achieve this unity, some kind of **repetition** of the first phrase would work well, but we don't want to simply repeat the whole of the first phrase again as this could sound a bit dull. We also need to end the second four-bar phrase on the key note of A in order to round off the section effectively.

For Practice

To complete the A section of our piece, try composing a second four-bar phrase to go along with the first. Remember that some kind of **repetition** of the first phrase will work, but you need to write some original music as well. You should also finish on the key note, A.

Now compare your newly composed four-bar phrase with mine. Notice that I've repeated the two-bar Question statement of the first four-bar phrase, but written a new two-bar Answer statement, finishing it off on the key note, A.

Now we have a complete A section, but we want to write a lively piece and, even if we play it fairly fast, so far our melody is a bit static because it moves in a similar rhythm all the way through.

We could try altering the rhythm or adding a few notes to give the phrase a bit more life, but adding extra notes might change the melody more than we would like. However, if we look for places where **passing notes** can be used we can liven up the rhythm as well as add notes without interfering with the basic melody too much.

For Practice

Study the eight bars of the A section written above (or your own version) and look for places where **passing notes** can be inserted. Try adding some to make the rhythm more interesting.

Here is my new version of the melody with passing notes added.

Now the section has greater rhythmic variety as well as an increased feeling of movement. However, the flow of this movement stops a little with the minims (half notes) midway through bars 2 and 4. So, ideally we need to add something at each of these points to keep the melody moving smoothly. We especially want to make the last two bars (bars 7 and 8) lively so that the A section finishes off well.

For Practice

Play through the A section (my version or your own) a few times – or have it played for you – and compose something to replace the longer minim notes at bars 2 and 4 that will help to keep the melody moving at these points. You need only use between one and three new notes in each bar, and remember to make sure that your new notes fit with everything else in the A section.

Here is my amended version of the A section.

You will see that I have halved the value of each minim to a crotchet in bars 2 and 4, and also added an **anacrusis** at the end of these bars. The idea for using an anacrusis was inspired by the new melody and rhythm created when I added passing notes in bar 3.

Notice also the pattern of the last four quavers in bar 6 and the first four quavers in bar 7. This is a type of **sequence** that can be very effective when used in **ascending** and **descending** melodies – which is what is happening here. (Oh, and I've changed the fifth note in bar 4 from a D to an E – just because I thought it sounded better!)

After playing through the melody a few more times, I decided to make one final alteration which seems to balance it out even more, and that was to add an **anacrusis** at the very start of the piece. (Doing this has given the A section a new bar number 1.)

Our structure plan now looks like this:

'A' SECTION

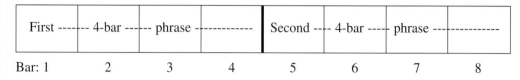

First ---	--- 4-bar ---	--- phrase -	-----------	Second --	-- 4-bar ---	- phrase ---	-----------
Bar: 1	2	3	4	5	6	7	8

'B' SECTION

Bars 9–16 ---

'A' SECTION

Repeat ---	- of first ---	- 4-bar ------	- phrase	Repeat ---	of second	- 4-bar --	phrase

Bars 17–24 --

Two-thirds of the piece are already complete! We just need to compose another eight bars of music now for the B section.

Contrast and development

The B section in a piece of music in ternary form ideally has to **contrast** with the A section.

A good way to provide contrast is to change the **dynamics** or the **key**, and normally when a piece of this kind begins in a major key (as this one does) it would **modulate** into a minor key.

Two possible options here are A minor (since the piece has started in A major) and F♯ minor (the **relative minor** key to A major). I will be using A minor as an example, but you can try F♯ minor if you wish.

Although the B section is mainly about contrast, we can also use it to **develop** some of the musical ideas from the A section. We have to ensure that there is not only contrast, but also some kind of *unity* between the B and A sections so that they don't end up sounding as though they aren't part of the same piece of music.

To achieve this we should look at what we have already composed and the ways new ideas might be created from that material.

Techniques for developing musical ideas

- Repeat a main **theme**, **motif**, or **section** of music that has been used before but in a different way. You could change its **key**, **rhythm** or **dynamics**, and perhaps also add some **variation**, **accents**, **staccato** or **syncopation**.

- Repeat some of the rhythms that have been used before but change the notes.

- A group of notes which have been played earlier in **ascending** order can be repeated in **descending** order (and vice versa).

- Print or write out your melody by hand in standard music notation and then turn the page upside down and try playing the 'new' notes. You might be pleasantly surprised by what you hear!

- Try playing a section of music backwards (reading from right to left).

- Experiment with **augmentation** and **diminution** (usually by doubling or halving the note lengths).

- Repeat small sections at a higher or lower pitch (you can develop this idea further by creating a **melodic sequence**).

- Break up a section of music into small fragments (single bars or even just a few notes) and move these around to hear what they sound like when played in a different order.

Look at the A section again now and pick out what you think are the strongest (or most memorable) musical features. These can be related to the melody or just the rhythm.

I think that the rhythm and **anacrusis** are the two strongest features of the section, so we might use these again in some way in the B section in order to achieve a sense of unity in the piece.

For Practice

Using the two musical features mentioned above (or two of your own), try composing eight bars of music (in the new minor key) for the B section now. If you prefer, you can choose to write completely contrasting music that has little or nothing in common with the A section, but if you do this you will have to be careful that your piece doesn't sound disjointed.

Here is my version of the B section. Look at it carefully and try to identify how I have built up the music from ideas already used in the A section.

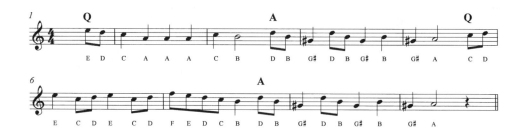

Now here is an analysis of my B section.

To lead into the B section I have kept the little **anacrusis** motif which was used throughout the A section, but to add some **variation** I have made the notes of the anacrusis **descend** this time – for example, the A section begins with the three notes C#, D, E, and the B section now begins with E, D, C.

I want to emphasise the new key of A minor, so the first complete bar of the B section (bar 2) contains notes found in the chord of A minor. That is why I have chosen the note C for beat 1, followed by a **pedal** of three A notes for beats 2, 3 and 4.

In bar 3 I have again begun with a C, but this time followed it with a longer note (a minim, B), which creates a slight pause in the music and suggests an **imperfect cadence** – both of which strengthen the effect of these two bars being a two-bar Question statement. (Using some longer note values in the B section will give the impression of a slower speed, and so create even more **contrast** with the A section.)

For the Answer statement, again I have used the **anacrusis** motif (at the end of bar 3), but altered it for more variety: this time I made the distance between the **pitch** of the notes in the **anacrusis** a little further apart (a third instead of a tone), creating a **leaping** melody rather than a **stepwise** melody. This three-note leaping motif is repeated in bar 4, and in bar 5 the notes G# followed by A create a **perfect cadence** which nicely rounds off the Answer statement – and so completes the first four-bar phrase of the B section.

For the next two-bar Question statement of the B section (end of bar 5 to bar 7) I chose to **repeat** the music first heard in bars 1–3 of the A section, but this time it appears in the new key of A minor and therefore has received some **variation**. For the two-bar Answer statement (end of bar 7 to finish) I have repeated the three-note leaping motif, and then finished off with G# to A to create a **perfect cadence**.

We're almost there! As the A section is to be repeated there's nothing much more to do, but it would be good to alter the end of the piece a little to create a stronger effect of completion. We could add a **coda**, which might be a few bars long, but we'd have to be careful not to upset the balance of the piece by doing this. Another option would be to simply alter the last couple of bars to make them sound more convincing as an ending.

For Practice

Look over/play through the whole ternary piece now (sections A, B, A) and decide whether you would like to change anything about it – in particular the repeated A section. You might want to alter some aspect of the **rhythm** or the **melody**, add a **coda**, or simply leave everything as it is. Remember that if you have access to music software you can do this exercise by keying the notes into a computer and then playing back the whole piece.

Below is my final version of the whole melody, now titled *Study in A,* and given the **tempo** of *allegro*.

Note: I decided to **repeat** the first A section (extending it to sixteen bars) as well as the B section (extending that to sixteen bars as well). I then altered the final two bars of the piece so that there is some **variation** in the second-last bar, and the three notes in the very last bar now ascend towards the key note of A followed by a crotchet rest to create a sudden, cheerful end to the piece.

For Practice

How would the final *structure plan* look now? Based on the music notation above (or your own version of the piece) draw a structure plan of the completed ternary form melody.

Adding additional parts to *Study in A*

We now have a good, well-balanced melody in ternary form.

To add accompanying parts to it such as chords, arpeggios and a bass line, we can use the techniques outlined in Inventing Workshop 1, but there is another kind of **counter-melody** we could use that would work well in this piece. It involves using the musical **intervals** of a third and a sixth. For example, the first note in bar 2 of *Study in A* is an E, so we could harmonise that note with the note a third *below*, which is C#, or the note a sixth *below*, which is G#.

By using these intervals of a third and a sixth we can build a counter-melody which closely harmonises with our melody.

Here are the first three bars of *Study in A* with a **counter-melody** written a third below the main melody. This type of counter-melody often has longer note values than the main melody to ensure that it doesn't interfere with it.

Hints and Tips

The method of writing a counter-melody using intervals of a third and a sixth is a helpful composing technique to use when writing a **descant** above a melody. In this case, the intervals of a third and a sixth *above* the main melody would be used to build the descant, probably with some passing notes also.

For Practice

Based on what has been covered in the last two workshops, try composing at least three additional parts to accompany *Study in A* and/or your own version of the piece, one of which should be a **counter-melody** using the intervals of a third and a sixth, and the other a bass part. For the remaining part(s) you might choose to add chords, arpeggios or an Alberti bass.

Experiment with different rhythms, but make sure that none of your additional parts are so busy that they drown out the main melody.

CD Track 76. Below is my completed version of *Study in A*, now in four parts, which you can hear on CD track 76. Notice that I have added a counter-melody using thirds and sixths (part 2); a counter-melody in a lower pitch which is mostly built around the rhythm ♪ ♩ . (part 3); and lastly a slow-moving bass part to add depth and establish the harmony in each bar.

INVENTING

Study in A

Joe McGowan

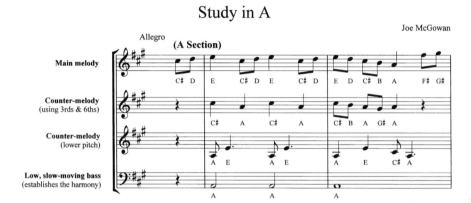

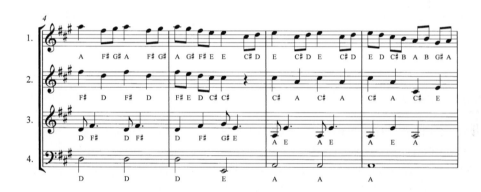

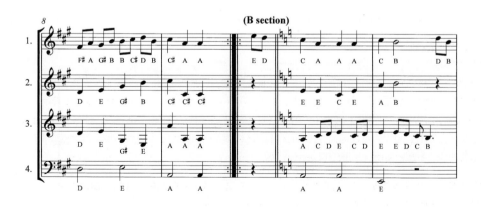

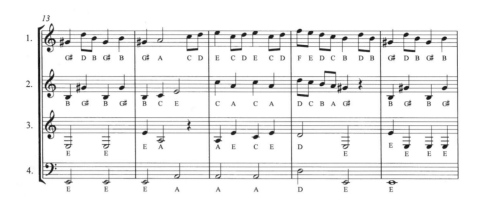

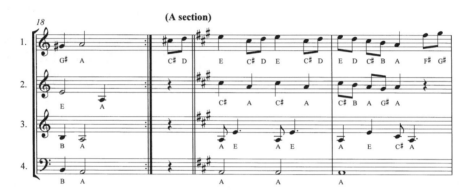

For Practice

Here are four fragments of music in different styles, speeds and keys – they will be the opening bars of four pieces which *you* will compose! Your job is to build a complete piece of music out of each one, using the composing techniques covered in Workshops 1 and 2. The form and length of each piece will be your choice, but remember to aim for a well-balanced structure in each case. Good luck!

Melody 1. Key: G Major

Melody 2. Key: C Major

Melody 3. Key: F Major

Melody 4. Key: B Minor

Hints and Tips

Remember, you don't need to compose music using any particular system. There are no 'laws' governing how you invent music but, like all the best composers, if you know how to make the most of your ideas by using techniques like those we have covered in the last two workshops, then the task can become easier – and more rewarding. The most important thing is to experiment and see what works for you – and above all, enjoy it!

Inventing Workshop 3: Improvising

Improvising music isn't just about playing the notes of a particular scale/key at random over a chord progression or a steady drum beat. Good improvising has a shape or structure; it 'speaks' through notes alone.

Unless you are improvising in the style of something like heavy metal or hard rock (where sequences of fast notes and scale passages are likely to be required), think of an improvisation as a song where the melody is 'sung' on your instrument without words or lyrics. You should therefore aim to shape phrases in much the same way as they occur in vocal music, thinking about Question-and-Answer phrases, pitch, rests, pauses, and using longer notes where a breath would be taken or where a phrase ends. Reviewing some of the techniques used in workshop 1 will help you with this.

A common mistake made by those inexperienced with improvising is using too many notes or trying to play too fast, both of which can make the music sound as though it has no structure or direction, and is 'jabbering' rather than speaking! Listen to the improvisations in slow blues or jazz music and how the instruments often seem to copy the way a singer would perform a melody, with phrases, pauses and rhythmic variety.

Tips for good improvising

◆ Use phrases of a similar length to those used in vocal music to create a 'singing' effect.

◆ Include rests and pauses.

◆ Vary the rhythm, but not too much – a lot of different rhythms can sometimes make the improvisation sound disjointed.

◆ Use **dynamics** (create some variation with quiet and louder passages).

◆ Use **ascending**, **descending**, **leaping** and **stepwise** melodies during the course of your improvisation.

- Try techniques such as **staccato**, **accents**, **ornaments**, **glissando**, **sequence**, **syncopation** and **imitation** – but use them sparingly! Trying to throw in everything all at once can make the music sound like a random hotchpotch of sounds that have no structure or direction, whereas the occasional appearance of a different technique every now and then sounds more relaxed, sophisticated and professional.

- Using some **repetition** will give your improvisation continuity and a sense of structure.

Improvising is normally carried out over a chord progression or some kind of **ostinato**. You can practise improvising by having a friend play a chord progression in a particular style, or an ostinato (such as a bass guitar **riff**) over which you improvise, paying attention to the speed and style of the accompaniment. But you can also record an ostinato, a riff, or a chord progression into a keyboard or computer yourself and then improvise over it as it is played back.

For Practice

Below are some chord progressions in different musical styles. Choose a suitable scale to improvise over each progression, then get a fellow musician to play the progressions for you (or record them yourself and play them back) while you improvise along with the accompaniment, following the tips for good improvising above.

If you are unsure about any of the styles, review them before recording them or having them played for you.

If you like what you come up with in the following exercises, you might want to record some of it as part of your Inventing or Performing assessment material. Just remember, when improvising music your instrument is a voice, so make what you are saying sound like an interesting story, not a boring lecture!

KEY: D major	TEMPO: Lento	STYLE: A slow song

```
4
4   D  |  D  |  G  |  G  |  D  |  D  |  A  |  A  :‖

‖:  D  |  D  |  G  |  G  |  A  |  A  |  D  |  D  :‖
```

For Practice continued ➤

For Practice *continued*

KEY: A major   TEMPO: Andante   STYLE: Waltz

$\frac{3}{4}$ A | A | E | E | D | A | E | E :‖

‖: A | A | F♯m | F♯m | D | E | A | A :‖

KEY: G major   TEMPO: Moderato   STYLE: 12-bar Blues

$\frac{4}{4}$ G | G | C | C | G | G | C | C |

D | C | G | D :‖

KEY: F major   TEMPO: Allegretto   STYLE: Brisk Scottish March

$\frac{2}{4}$ F | Dm | F | C | F | Dm | B♭ | C :‖

‖: B♭ | Dm | B♭ | C | F | Dm | C | F :‖

KEY: A minor   TEMPO: Allegro   STYLE: Jig

$\frac{6}{8}$ Am | Am | Dm | Am | Am | Dm | F | E :‖

‖: Am | Am | F | Am | Am | Dm | E | Am :‖

Inventing Workshop 4: Arranging

Arranging music can be great fun. And since any piece you might want to arrange has been composed already, you need only concern yourself with experimenting with changes to the **rhythm**, **tempo**, **key**, **harmony** etc, or adding extra parts to be played by different instruments.

An arrangement can simply involve choosing a suitable combination of instruments to play the piece, or a complete re-work involving unusual sound-effects and harmony which transforms the music entirely.

You might consider arranging

◆ a favourite pop song

◆ a traditional song (a folk song or a Scots ballad)

◆ a song from a collection of popular songs

◆ a short instrumental work (such as *Study in A* from Instrumental Workshop 2)

◆ a piece for a solo instrument (which you harmonise and then arrange for several instruments).

A good way to practise arranging and experimenting with various sounds and effects is to choose a fairly simple piece of music and record it into your computer (doing this either with a midi keyboard or by inserting the notes using the computer's mouse). This will allow you to hear what the piece will sound like when played by different instruments and instrumental combinations, since you can play lots of sounds (or tracks) at the same time using music software.

After that you can add chords, a counter-melody, a bass part or whatever you feel the piece needs. Alternatively, you can get some fellow musicians who play different instruments to help you with this experimental work.

For Practice

CD Track 77. Below is the melody of a short piece of music in the key of D major, titled *Lullaby*, which you can hear on CD track 77. Listen to the piece a few times and then begin arranging it in a way which you feel will make it sound more complete. You could think about adding **lyrics**, basic **chords** (from which you might create an **arpeggio** style accompaniment), a **counter-melody**, a **descant**, a **bass part**, or certain combinations of these (referring back to Inventing Workshops 1 and 2 will help you with this). Last of all, choose instruments which will suit the **style** of the piece and the kind of accompanying parts you compose. You should think about which instruments are best suited to play each part in terms of their sound and technical capabilities. Which instruments would suit the style of the *Lullaby* but also sound good together? Which can sustain long notes? Which are better suited to play arpeggios?

For Practice continued ➤

For Practice continued

For Practice continued ➤

For Practice continued

Listening to different instrumental combinations such as those used in folk groups, jazz groups, and various quartet groups might give you some ideas. You may want to change the piece even more by re-recording it at a different speed, or with some of the notes and rhythms altered. It will be your arrangement so the choice is yours!

Hints *and* Tips

When you have finished arranging *Lullaby*, you will have another piece of music that could be included as part of your Inventing or (if you record it with other students) Group Performing assessment material.

PERFORMING

As part of your Standard Grade Music course you are required to play **two** different musical instruments. You will have the choice to perform solo on both of those instruments, or solo on one, and as a member of a group on the other.

Depending on the resources at your school, you can normally choose two instruments from the following selection:

accordion	piano
bagpipes	violin
trumpet	fiddle
French horn	viola
trombone	cello
tuba	double bass
drum kit	flute
snare drum	oboe
tuned percussion (timpani, glockenspiel, xylophone etc.)	clarinet
	saxophone
guitar (classical or acoustic)	bassoon
bass guitar	recorder
harp (including clarsach)	voice
keyboard	

Since the performing component of Standard Grade Music is a practical activity that does not involve any written work, this chapter only provides a review of the most important points relating to this part of your course; these include practical advice on practising, performing and coping with exam nerves, as well as tips on how to approach your final solo performing exam. (In any case, your teacher and instrumental instructor – if you have one – will guide you in this area.)

General advice on practising

◆ Get into a daily practice routine. Regular practice is the key to playing well consistently. Twenty minutes' practice **every day** is better than an hour every other day, or cramming in several hours the day before your music lesson.

Above all, don't think that you can leave all the practice until the weeks leading up to your solo performing exam and then go at it like mad – you won't play your best if you do that.

◆ Practising should be enjoyable, not a slog. You don't have to lock yourself in your room every night for a gruelling session. Varying the way you practise, perhaps by splitting up the session into a couple of different things, is a good way to keep yourself motivated.

◆ Recording your pieces is a good idea. You can then play them back and listen to yourself, which will allow you to note any aspects of your playing that could do with improvement. Recording yourself is also good exam practice because you will be concentrating fully on playing your very best – just as you will need to in the exam!

◆ If you don't have much time to practise, perhaps because of other homework commitments, at least try to get fifteen minutes in. Half a practice session is better than none at all.

◆ Regular practice will help you to perform well in front of an examiner. If you haven't practised as much as you could have, any weaknesses in your playing will come out whenever you feel tense.

Solo performing tips

◆ Try to get as much experience as possible playing in front of others. This can include your family, fellow students, friends – even strangers if you can persuade them to listen!

◆ If your playing falls apart near the **start** of a piece, don't panic; just apologise and begin again. This is better than fumbling around until you get back on track, because then you will have made a poor opening impression.

◆ If you make a mistake **further on** in the piece, do your best to **carry on playing**, because if you flinch, groan, apologise or, worst of all, stop playing, you will only draw more attention to your error and therefore make it bigger. If you are reading from printed music and you lose your place, pick up the music from a point close to where things went wrong and carry on.

◆ If you give a poor performance, don't mope about it too much afterwards; this will only make you feel less confident about next time. Rather than allowing a dodgy performance to put you off, perform again as soon as possible. No one plays their best every time, and sometimes we even need the odd weak performance to motivate ourselves to improve. The important thing is to get lots of experience playing in front of others, not to get a standing ovation every time you play!

Performance nerves

◆ The fear of making mistakes because of performance nerves is something which causes most of us apprehension about playing in front of people. But one of the first steps towards controlling this fear is to **accept that you are probably going to be a little nervous**. Don't let the feeling take you by surprise. If you do, it has the upper hand. If you *expect* the nerves, you are prepared – and that is the first step towards coping with them.

◆ You can use performance nerves to your advantage: being a little nervous will help you to stay alert and focused on your playing.

◆ Playing in front of others as often as you can gives you lots of practice at experiencing that nervy feeling. You will then become more accustomed to the sensation and learn how to play while feeling like this.

◆ You are unlikely to play as well in front of others as you do when practising in your bedroom with absolutely no pressure on you whatsoever. Performing is different from practising, so don't expect to magically conquer nervousness, even if you perform a lot in front of people, because it is perfectly natural, even beneficial, to feel those butterflies!

Just before your Solo Performing exam

◆ Make sure you know the exact time and place of your exam and make arrangements to ensure you get there in plenty of time. Running late on the day of the exam is a sure way to put yourself under a lot of pressure before you go in.

◆ Go to bed early the night before your exam to ensure you get plenty of sleep. A lack of rest will affect your powers of concentration and can make you feel stressed.

The day of the exam

◆ Eat something sensible on the day of your exam because some foods won't help your mood or concentration. Fruit, cereals and orange juice for breakfast will help to keep you alert, but tea and coffee aren't so good since the caffeine in them can make you feel a little edgy or tense, and even makes some people shake. Drinking water is especially important if you are going to be singing.

◆ Have a warm-up before going in to your exam, but don't play (or sing) for too long – this can put you 'off the boil'.

◆ Do you know how things are going to be set up in the exam room? Where are you going to position yourself? If you are using an accompanist, where will he/she be sitting? You can ask your teacher about these things beforehand.

The Solo Performing exam

◆ When you go into the exam room don't be in a rush to begin playing. Take a little time to get comfortable and position your music (if you are reading from it) so that you can see it clearly.

◆ Remind yourself that you have put in lots of practice for the exam … then decide that you are going to prove this to the examiner!

◆ Don't worry if you make a mistake or two during the performance. The examiner knows you are likely to be nervous and expects that students will make some performance errors. Even professional players make mistakes sometimes, and you are not a professional, so the examiner won't be expecting perfection from you – but don't let that stop you trying to achieve it!

◆ The examiner will be impressed if you keep on playing in the event that you make a mistake. This shows that you are in control, and have a professional approach to playing.

◆ Allowing a single mistake to bother you is a sure way to upset your concentration, which could easily cause you to make further mistakes. So don't worry about the occasional blunder. In most cases these will sound much worse to you than they actually are.

◆ Remember, even the best players make mistakes. It will be the parts you play well that the examiner will take into account when marking you.

◆ The examiner will enjoy what you are playing if you commit yourself to playing with feeling; this is more important than playing without making a single mistake, so don't be scared to let go and put everything into the music.

◆ Don't forget that copies of the music you will be playing have to be given to the examiner.

Hints and Tips

Examiners want to give you the best mark they can. They want you to pass. They also understand that you will be nervous, so don't feel worried about the fact that you might *appear* nervous. The examiners have been there too so they know what you are going through!

Group Performing

If you choose the Group Performing option, you will be required to record some of your performances when playing with other musicians from your Standard Grade Music class. A group can consist of between two and eight players, and your teacher will guide you on recording your performances and choosing your best recordings for assessment.

Important points about group performing

◆ Be patient with other members of your group. Your job is to work together as a team to make good music (and enjoy it), so bad tempers or big-headed players will only cause problems – which will affect the music itself.

◆ Organise regular rehearsals and make sure every group member knows his/her responsibilities – for example, which music or equipment to bring along.

◆ When recording a piece for your assessment material, make sure that you can be heard very clearly on the recording. This is the most important thing, even though the group may sound a bit unbalanced as a result.

◆ Copies of the music you have recorded for assessment also need to be presented along with your recording.

◆ Your final grade for Group Performing will depend upon your best recorded performances, as well as your attitude as a group member. The assessment will be carried out by your class teacher during the course, and all work for this section normally has to be completed by April of the exam year.

REFERENCE PAGES

Voice ranges

From highest (soprano) to lowest (bass):

Soprano (high female voice)

Mezzo-soprano (female voice between soprano and alto)

Alto (low female voice)

Counter-tenor (high or 'falsetto' male voice between tenor and alto)

Tenor (high male voice)

Baritone (male voice between bass and tenor)

Bass (low male voice)

(Soprano, Alto, Tenor and Bass voices ('SATB') are standard for most choirs)

Musical instruments

Orchestral instruments

The orchestra is split into four groups or 'families' of instruments (shown below). Instruments in brackets are not always used in the orchestra, but may be required for certain pieces.

Woodwind

In this family of instruments the sound is produced by **blowing**. A technique used by them is **flutter-tonguing**.

Instruments: (**Piccolo**), **Flute**, **Oboe**, (**Cor Anglais**), **Clarinet**, (**Bass Clarinet**), (**Saxophone**), **Bassoon**, (**Double Bassoon**)

Strings

For the violin, viola, cello and double bass the sound is produced by **bowing** (**arco**) or **plucking** (**pizzicato**). Techniques used are **col legno**, **con sordino**, **vibrato**, **double stopping** and **tremolando** or **tremolo**. The harp is **plucked** or **strummed** and can use **double stopping** and **tremolo** techniques.

Instruments: **Violin** (in two groups: *first* and *second*), **Viola**, **Cello**, **Double bass**, (**Harp**)

Brass

In this family of instruments the sound is produced by **blowing**. A technique used by them is **con sordino**.

Instruments: **Trumpet, French horn, Trombone, Tuba**

Percussion

In this family of instruments the sound is produced by **striking** – this is done using sticks, beaters, the hand, or by striking two instruments together (as with cymbals and castanets).

Many different *tuned* and *untuned* percussion instruments can be used depending on the piece being performed, but these are the most common:

Tuned percussion

Timpani

Glockenspiel

Xylophone

Tubular bells

Untuned percussion

Gong

Side drum

Bass drum

Triangle

Wood block

Tambourine

Cymbals

 ## *Keyboard instruments*

Piano, Organ, Harpsichord, Keyboard, Synthesiser

Folk instruments

Bagpipes, **Uillean pipes**, **Banjo**, **Clarsach**, **Accordion**, **Fiddle**, **Whistle** (penny whistle), **Bodhran**, **Guitar**

Guitars

Acoustic guitar, **Classical guitar**, **Electric guitar**, **12-string guitar**, **Bass guitar**, **Fretless bass**, **Slide guitar**

Ethnic instruments

Sitar – a large acoustic Indian instrument which resembles a guitar with a very long neck. It has twenty moveable frets and seven main strings underneath which are around twelve more 'sympathetic' strings tuned by pegs along the fingerboard.

Panpipes – a hand-held instrument consisting of different lengths of pipes, the tops of which are blown into while the other ends are stopped. An ancient instrument still used in the folk music of certain countries including South America (especially the Andes), Romania and Burma.

Note values and their rests

Semibreve or *Whole Note*	Dotted Minim or *Dotted Half Note*	Minim or *Half Note*	Crotchet or *Quarter Note*	Quaver or *Eighth Note*	Semiquaver or *Sixteenth Note*
𝅝	𝅗𝅥.	𝅗𝅥	𝅘𝅥	𝅘𝅥𝅮	𝅘𝅥𝅯
Sounds for **4 Crotchet** beats	Sounds for **3 Crotchet** beats	Sounds for **2 Crotchet** beats	Sounds for **1 Crotchet** beat	Sounds for **½ Crotchet** beat	Sounds for **¼ Crotchet** beat
Its rest is:	Its rest is:	Its rest is:	Its rest is:	Its rest is:	Its rest is:
▬	▬·	▬	𝄽	𝄾	𝄿

Dynamics

Symbol	Italian Word	Meaning
pp	pianissimo	very quiet
p	piano	quiet
mp	mezzo piano	moderately quiet
mf	mezzo forte	moderately loud
f	forte	loud
ff	fortissimo	very loud
	crescendo or *cresc.*	becoming louder
	diminuendo or *dim.*	becoming quieter

Tempo

A lot of modern music gives the precise speed that the composer or arranger intended the piece to be played at by indicating the metronome speed of the main beat at the start of the music. (A metronome is a mechanical or electronic device which can be set to sound a consistent number of loud clicks or bleeps at a precise speed. Metronomes are used both to let musicians hear the speed at which a piece should be played and as a guide to ensure they keep to that speed as they practise.)

 = 120 means there are exactly one hundred and twenty **crotchet** beats per minute.

 = 55 means there are exactly fifty-five **minim** beats per minute.

However, the more conventional system of using Italian words to indicate the intended speed of a piece of music is also used. Below is a list of some of the most common ones.

Italian word	Meaning
presto	very fast
vivace	fast, lively
allegro	rather fast, lively
allegretto	a little slower than *allegro*
moderato	moderately
andante	at a walking pace
adagio	slowly
lento	very slowly
accelerando	becoming faster
ritardando *rallentando* *ritenuto*	becoming slower
rubato	not in a strict beat; flexible time

Time signatures and rhythmic groupings

Below are some time signatures and the rhythms commonly used with them.

Simple time

2/4 time – two crotchet (or quarter) beats in a bar – often used for **marches**

3/4 time – three crotchet (or quarter) beats in a bar – often used for **waltzes**

4/4 time – four crotchet (or quarter) beats in a bar (also called 'common time' because it is used in a lot of music)

Compound time

6/8 time – six quaver (or eighth) beats in a bar – often used for **jigs**

1,2,3,4,5,6   1,2,3 4,5 6   1   2   3   4   5   6   1,2 3   4,5,6   1 & 2 & 3 & 4   5   6

9/8 time – nine quaver (or eighth) beats in a bar – sometimes used for **jigs**

1,2,3 4   5   6   7,8,9 1   2   3   4   5   6   7   8   9   1 & 2 & 3 & 4,5 6   7   8   9

12/8 time – twelve quaver (or eighth) beats in a bar

1, 2,3 4   5   6   7,8   9   10,11,12 1   2   3   4   5   6   7 & 8 & 9 & 10,11 12

Common keys and their chords

Key signature   Major key   Relative minor key

C major   **A minor**

Common chords in the key of **C major**

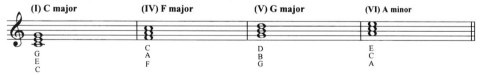

| (I) C major | (IV) F major | (V) G major | (VI) A minor |
| G E C | C A F | D B G | E C A |

Common chords in the key of **A minor**

| (I) A minor | (IV) D minor | (V) E minor | (VI) F major |
| E C A | A F D | B G# E | C A F |

Common 'sharp' keys

Key signature   Major key   Relative minor key

   **G major**   **E minor**

Common chords in the key of **G major**

(I) G major
D
B
G

(IV) C major
G
E
C

(V) D major
A
F#
D

(VI) E minor
B
G
E

Common chords in the key of **E minor**

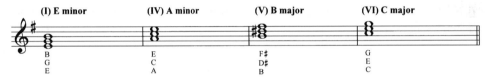

(I) E minor
B
G
E

(IV) A minor
E
C
A

(V) B major
F#
D#
B

(VI) C major
G
E
C

Key signature   Major key   Relative minor key

D major   **B minor**

Common chords in the key of **D major**

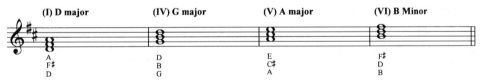

(I) D major
A
F#
D

(IV) G major
D
B
G

(V) A major
E
C#
A

(VI) B Minor
F#
D
B

Common chords in the key of **B minor**

(I) B minor
F#
D
B

(IV) E minor
B
G
E

(V) F# major
C#
A#
F#

(VI) G major
D
B
G

Key signature Major key Relative minor key

A major **F♯ minor**

Common chords in the key of **A major**

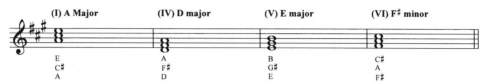

(I) A Major	(IV) D major	(V) E major	(VI) F♯ minor
E	A	B	C♯
C♯	F♯	G♯	A
A	D	E	F♯

Common chords in the key of **F♯ minor**

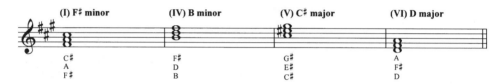

(I) F♯ minor	(IV) B minor	(V) C♯ major	(VI) D major
C♯	F♯	G♯	A
A	D	E♯	F♯
F♯	B	C♯	D

Key signature Major key Relative minor key

E major **C♯ minor**

Common chords in the key of **E major**

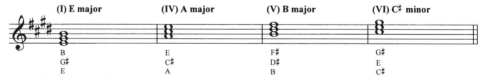

(I) E major	(IV) A major	(V) B major	(VI) C♯ minor
B	E	F♯	G♯
G♯	C♯	D♯	E
E	A	B	C♯

Common chords in the key of **C♯ minor**

(I) C♯ minor	(IV) F♯ minor	(V) G♯ major	(VI) A major
G♯	C♯	D♯	E
E	A	B♯	C♯
C♯	F♯	G♯	A

Common 'flat' keys

Key signature	Major key	Relative minor key
	**F major**	**D minor**

Common chords in the key of **F major**

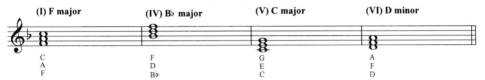

(I) F major	(IV) B♭ major	(V) C major	(VI) D minor
C A F	F D B♭	G E C	A F D

Common chords in the key of **D minor**

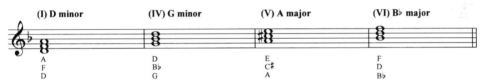

(I) D minor	(IV) G minor	(V) A major	(VI) B♭ major
A F D	D B♭ G	E C♯ A	F D B♭

Key signature	Major key	Relative minor key
	**B♭ major**	**G minor**

Common chords in the key of **B♭ major**

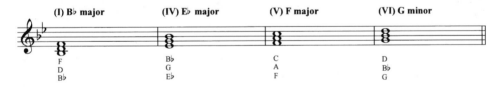

(I) B♭ major	(IV) E♭ major	(V) F major	(VI) G minor
F D B♭	B♭ G E♭	C A F	D B♭ G

Common chords in the key of **G minor**

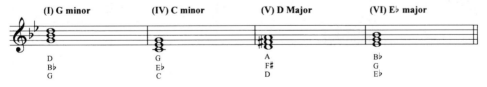

(I) G minor	(IV) C minor	(V) D Major	(VI) E♭ major
D B♭ G	G E♭ C	A F♯ D	B♭ G E♭

Key signature

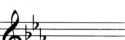

Major key

E♭ major

Relative minor key

C minor

Common chords in the key of **E♭ major**

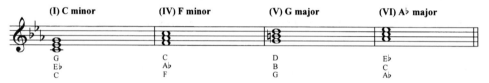

(I) E♭ major	(IV) A♭ major	(V) B♭ major	(VI) C minor
B♭	E♭	F	G
G	C	D	E♭
E♭	A♭	B♭	C

Common chords in the key of **C minor**

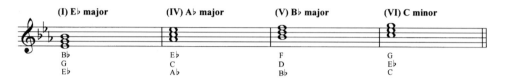

(I) C minor	(IV) F minor	(V) G major	(VI) A♭ major
G	C	D	E♭
E♭	A♭	B	C
C	F	G	A♭

Key signature

Major key

A♭ major

Relative minor key

F minor

Common chords in the key of **A♭ major**

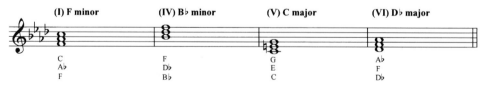

(I) A♭ major	(IV) D♭ major	(V) E♭ major	(VI) F minor
E♭	A♭	B♭	C
C	F	G	A♭
A♭	D♭	E♭	F

Common chords in the key of **F minor**

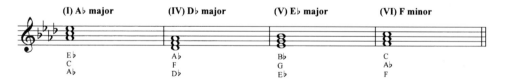

(I) F minor	(IV) B♭ minor	(V) C major	(VI) D♭ major
C	F	G	A♭
A♭	D♭	E	F
F	B♭	C	D♭

GLOSSARY OF MUSICAL CONCEPTS

1: Melody – Foundation level

Ascending melody – a tune which becomes higher in pitch as it progresses.

Descending melody – a tune which becomes lower in pitch as it progresses.

Stepwise melody – a tune which progresses in small steps rather than big jumps.

Leaping melody – a tune which progresses in big jumps.

Glissando – to slide smoothly between two notes which are some distance apart, with all the notes in between being played very rapidly.

Repetition – a passage or section of music which is repeated.

Theme – the main tune in a piece of music.

Question – a small phrase of music (which may be as short as two bars) which needs to be completed with an 'Answer' phrase.

Answer – a small phrase of music (which may be as short as two bars) which sounds as if it is 'answering' the previous phrase (the 'Question').

Section – can mean a particular part in a piece of music (for example, the middle section) or a group within the orchestra (for example, the string section).

Sequence – a passage of music which repeats at a higher or lower pitch.

Contrast – when the music changes key, speed, mood, volume etc.

Broken chord – when the notes of a chord are played separately rather than together.

1: Melody – General level

In addition to the above Melody concepts, you should also understand the following:

Phrase – a group of notes whose effect is like a small statement (like a sentence – or part of a sentence – in language).

Imitation – when a musical phrase in one part is copied (imitated) in another part.

Variation – when a melody or a whole section of music is changed in some way when it is repeated.

Ornament – extra 'decorative' notes added to a melody.

Scale – a rising or falling succession of notes consisting of the different notes found in a particular key or mode (for example, G A B C D E F♯ in the scale of G major).

Major scale – a scale whose order of tones and semitones makes a pleasant or 'happy' sound (for example, C major: C D E F G A B C) – from this we also get major chords and major intervals.

Minor scale – a scale whose order of tones and semitones makes a serious or 'sad' sound (for example, C minor: C D E♭ F G A♭ B) – from this we also get minor chords and minor intervals.

Chromatic scale – a scale which moves only in semitones (C C♯ D D♯ E F F♯ G G♯ A A♯ B C).

Diatonic scale – any scale made up of five tones and two semitones, such as the major scale, the natural minor scale and the seven basic modes.

Whole-tone scale – a scale which moves only in tones (for example, C D E F♯ G♯ B♭ C).

Pentatonic scale – a scale which uses only five different notes (and no semitones) to make a particular sound: for example, C E♭ F G B♭. Used in rock, jazz, blues and folk music.

Blues scale – a scale based on the pentatonic scale but with the addition of two extra 'blue' notes (semitones which create brief discord), for example C E♭ F **F♯** G B♭ C **C♯**. Used in blues music.

Grace note – a musical 'ornament': a rapid additional note used to decorate a melody.

1: Melody – Credit level

In addition to the above Melody concepts, you should also understand the following:

Relative major – a major key which is related to a minor key because it has the same key signature (all minor keys have relative major keys).

Relative minor – a minor key which is related to a major key because it has the same key signature (all major keys have relative minor keys).

Modal music – music which is not in a major or minor key but has its own fixed order of tones and semitones. All the white keys on the piano keyboard are used to make different modes. First used in medieval music.

Tonal music – music which uses a specific key (or keys) and therefore has a key note.

Atonal music – music which does not have a specific key but uses any note freely.

Semitone – the musical interval (the distance between two notes) of half a tone. This is the smallest distance between two notes in tonal music; each note on the piano keyboard is a semitone apart from the next note.

Tone – a musical interval made up of two semitones.

Modulation – when music changes from one key into another.

Contrary motion – notes or passages of music moving in opposite directions.

Interval – the distance between two notes. For example, C to G is a fifth; G to B is a third.

Inversion – when the notes of a chord are rearranged so that the root note is no longer the lowest note (for example, G C E or E G C instead of C E G in the chord of C major).

Register – a particular pitch range of a group of notes, instrument or voice (e.g. a high register for the violin would be notes which use ledger lines above the treble stave

2: Rhythm – Foundation level

Accent – a musical symbol > written above or below notes or chords which are to be played slightly louder.

Accented – a musical note, phrase, chord or passage which contains accents.

Rhythm – the different lengths (durations) of musical notes combined together in a piece of music.

Beat – the steady main pulse in a piece of music.

Bar – the 'compartments' on the musical stave which separate notes into a set number of beats e.g. two beats per bar, four beats per bar etc.

Syncopation – where the accent is off the main beat and on a weaker beat (the upbeat, for example).

March – a musical composition in duple metre (two main beats per bar) intended to be marched to.

Strathspey – a traditional Scottish dance reel in 4/4 time with a moderate tempo and characterised by a dotted rhythm.

Reel – a lively Scottish dance in duple meter (two beats per bar) which often moves in fast, smooth quavers. Also common in Ireland and North America.

Jig – a fast dance found in Scottish and Irish folk music, normally in 6/8 time.

Waltz – a dance in moderate tempo triple metre (three beats per bar).

Pause (fermata) – a musical symbol 🎵 written over a note, chord or rest to indicate that the player(s) should pause at that point.

a tempo – return to the original speed.

On the beat – where the stress or accent is on the main beat(s).

Off the beat – where the stress or accent is off the main beat (on the upbeat, for example – as in syncopation).

2: Rhythm – General level

In addition to the above Rhythm concepts, you should also understand the following:

Simple time – a time signature where the main beats are divisible by two, for example crotchets in 2/4, 3/4 or 4/4 time, or minims in 2/2 time.

Compound time – a time signature where the main beats are divisible by three, for example dotted quavers in 6/8, 9/8 or 12/8 time.

Unaccented – a musical note, chord or passage which does not have an accent.

Upbeat – the weaker beat which comes before the strong downbeat.

Downbeat – the strong beat at the beginning of a bar.

Anacrusis – the upbeat note (or notes) before the first strong beat of a bar.

Lead-in – a short passage of music – or perhaps just a note or two (see **anacrusis**) – which leads into the main tune.

Speed variations (tempo variations) – speeding up or slowing down from the original speed; indicated by, for example, *accelerando*, *rallentando*, *ritenuto*, or *ritardando*; also *rubato* (flexibility of time). (See Tempo, page 92–93.)

Scotch snap – a rhythm where a short note on the beat is followed by a longer one (for example, 🎵 .); often used in Scottish music.

Sforzando – where a note or chord is played with a very strong or loud accent.

2: Rhythm – Credit level

In addition to the above Rhythm concepts, you should also understand the following:

Rhythmic groupings in simple and compound time – see the section on time signatures and rhythmic groupings on pages 93–94.

Cross rhythms – where the normal accents of a time signature are moved around to create different kinds of rhythms in a piece of music, or when separate parts play different rhythms at the same time.

3: Style – Foundation level

Pop – a style of music which uses modern sounds and song lyrics (words) that are normally popular with the mass public, particularly the younger generation.

Rock – a popular modern style of music which developed from Rock 'n' Roll. Rock music often uses 'heavier' lyrics and more driving beats than pop music, even though both styles use electric instruments, drums and amplified singing.

Rock 'n' Roll – a style of dance music from mid-1950s America which developed from rhythm-and-blues. Elvis Presley was one of the most famous Rock 'n' Roll singers of all time.

Reggae – originally appearing in Jamaica in the mid 1960s, reggae is now a popular style of urban dance music, characterised by accented upbeats or off-beats (syncopation).

Latin-American – a style which blends different kinds of music from several cultures, including Spain, the Caribbean and South America; one of its most popular versions is lively South American jazz.

Ragtime – a style of popular American music from the early 1900s, characterised by lively, often syncopated melodies in strict rhythm. Most ragtime pieces were written for piano, and many of the more famous examples were composed by Scott Joplin (including *The Entertainer* and *Maple Leaf Rag*).

Swing – a style of lively popular jazz and big band dance music which first appeared in the 1930s. Pieces by Glenn Miller are among the most famous in this style, as are songs sung by Ella Fitzgerald.

Negro spiritual – a style of folk singing dating from the eighteenth century, associated with the African-American churches of the Deep South and sometimes with black slavery.

Jazz – an improvised style of music developed by African-Americans in the early twentieth century which often uses lively swing rhythms and bent pitches (discordant notes used to 'colour' the music).

Blues – an improvised African-American folk music whose name refers to the often melancholy nature of the music and the 'blue' (discordant) notes used. Blues is based on chord progressions which last for eight, twelve or thirty-two bars (the most common being twelve-bar blues) over which a melody normally based on the blues scale is played or sung.

Scottish – music linked closely with Scotland and traditional (early) Scottish styles such as the reel, jig, strathspey, mouth music, bothy ballad etc.

Folk – a style in which the lyrics (words) and music reflect aspects of the culture and traditions of a country. The folk revival of recent times has seen an increase in the popularity of traditional folk music as well as new music in the style (Capercaillie and Runrig are among the modern Scottish folk revival groups).

3: Style – General level

In addition to the above Style concepts, you should also understand the following:

Baroque – a term used to describe music from about 1600–1750 which is characterised by features such as contrast (contrasting dynamics, tempo etc.), walking bass and ornaments. Famous baroque composers include J. S. Bach, Handel and Vivaldi.

Samba – highly syncopated African-Brazilian dance music in duple metre (two beats per bar).

Salsa – a style of lively music from Cuba which appeared in the 1940s, Salsa music is still popular dance music in many countries.

Romantic – the term used to describe the musical style of the nineteenth century when composers such as Mahler, Wagner and Tchaikowsky created music which explored human feelings and experiences in greater depth than ever before. The music varied from dreamy, romantic or tranquil (piano miniatures by Chopin and Schumann) to the very loud and powerful (Wagner operas and orchestral works by Holst).

Dixieland – an early style of traditional jazz music from the USA played by white musicians of the so-called New Orleans school.

'Scat' singing – a style of jazz singing where meaningless words or syllables are sung over improvised music.

Vamp – improvising a simple chord accompaniment (normally on the piano) to a solo.

3: Style – Credit level

In addition to the above Style concepts, you should also understand the following:

Aleatoric – a twentieth-century term which describes music in which some or all parts of the composition or performance are left to chance. For example, dice might be rolled to determine which bar numbers will contain a particular melody, or the player might be allowed the freedom to play a set of given notes in any order or rhythm.

Boogie-woogie – a blues piano style from the early twentieth century characterised by a repetitive bass rhythm (played by the left hand) over which an improvised melody is played (with the right hand).

Classical – the term used to describe music which is not part of folk or popular traditions, as well as music from the late eighteenth to early nineteenth centuries where careful attention to detail, formal structures (such as the sonata and symphony) and general high standards of musical excellence characterise the music of composers including Haydn, Mozart and Beethoven.

Minimalist – a term first used in the early 1970s to describe music which uses simple, repetitive melodies and rhythms that are gradually extended by adding more and more of these simple 'layers' of music until a more complex structure develops.

Soul music – a style of popular music from African-American musicians since the early 1960s where the performer displays strong and sincere emotions through a very expressive singing style.

Impressionism – a style, first appearing in the 1870s, where the expression of a mood (often dreamy and romantic) or an emotion is the most important aspect, and musical structures and chord progressions are looser.

Neo-classical – a term describing a twentieth-century style where some composers (for example, Stravinsky, Schoenberg and Prokofiev) wrote music in the earlier style of classical music.

Serialism – a technique first used by Schoenberg in the early 1920s in which one or more musical elements in a piece of music (note pitches, dynamics, etc.) are ordered into a fixed 'series'.

Gospel – a style of religious singing which began in 1850s America in the Protestant evangelical church and which, in the twentieth century, became a popular song category not linked with religion.

Musique concrète – a term first used in the late 1940s by electronic music composers in Paris to describe 'concrete' sounds that are recorded (rather than being written down as musical notation that has to be performed later).

Passion – a piece which portrays the story of the crucifixion of Jesus Christ. Over the centuries there have been several versions of this style, but its largest is an orchestral work with chorus and soloists; Bach's *St John Passion* and *St Matthew Passion* are considered the finest examples.

Country – a style of popular American folk music which was first played in rural communities at functions or in the home (using fiddles, banjos and guitars) but later expanded into a large industry where the style was developed by performers such as Willie Nelson, Patsy Cline, Dolly Parton and Johnny Cash.

Indian – all styles of Indian music, which include vocal music, Indian classical music and instrumental styles. Indian melodies are formed using special scales/modes called ragas and various set rhythmic patterns known as talas.

Atonal – a twentieth-century term describing music that is not tonal (is not in a key) and can freely use any note; Schoenberg, Webern and Berg wrote the earliest atonal pieces.

4: Timbre – Foundation level

Staccato – short, detached notes or chords.

Legato – smooth notes or chords with no silences in between (the opposite of staccato).

Double stopping – playing two notes at the same time on a stringed instrument such as violin, cello or guitar.

Sound – any noise which can be detected by the ears as it travels on the airwaves which surround us. Music is a collection of various 'noises' produced by musicians in order to create particular sounds and pitches.

Silence – the absence of sound.

Sustained – sound which is held on to continue in a steady, unbroken flow.

Striking – when an instrument is hit (with the hand or a beater – such as a drumstick) to produce a sound.

Blowing – the method of producing sound on any wind instrument (for example, flute, trumpet or recorder) by using the breath.

Bowing – the method of producing sound on a string instrument (such as violin, viola, cello or double bass) by drawing a bow over the strings.

Strumming – a method of producing sound on string instruments such as the guitar and banjo by quickly drawing the fingers or a plectrum (a small triangular shaped object) across the strings.

Plucking – a method of producing sound on any string instrument with the fingers or (on guitars and banjo) a plectrum.

Slapping – a technique used on string instruments such as guitar and (especially) bass guitar where the strings are slapped to produce a particular sound.

Muted/muting – dampening the sound produced by an instrument to make it quieter; this can be done with the hand on some instruments (such as guitar and French horn), or by using a special device known as a mute (on orchestral stringed instruments and brass instruments).

Orchestra – a large group of musicians who play a selection of instruments grouped into four main 'families': woodwind, brass, percussion and strings. Music can be either written especially for orchestra (as with a symphony) or arranged for it, but in all cases the orchestra is directed by a conductor who dictates the speed, dynamics and overall interpretation of a piece, and generally makes sure everyone plays well together.

Pipe band – a Scottish marching band where only bagpipes and drums are played.

Wind/military band – a band of woodwind, brass and percussion musicians who often play brisk military music including marches (such as those by John Philip Sousa).

Brass band – a band in which different kinds of brass instruments such as trumpet, cornet, horn and euphonium are played.

Steel band – a group of musicians who play tuned percussion instruments which are made from oil drums. These bands began in the 1930s in the West Indies.

Big band – a style of lively jazz dance music played by a large group of musicians. The music of Benny Goodman, Duke Ellington and the Count Basie orchestra represents the big band style.

Scottish dance band – a group, often consisting of piano, accordion, fiddle and drums, who play traditional Scottish music.

Pop group – a band of musicians who play pop music, normally using a singer (or singers), electric and bass guitars, drums and possibly keyboard.

Folk group – a band of musicians who play folk music; in Scottish folk music such a group might play instruments such as fiddle, penny whistle, accordion and guitar.

Rock group – a band who play rock music, normally on electric and bass guitars, drums, vocals and possibly keyboard.

Jazz group – a band of musicians who play jazz music on instruments which can include piano, saxophone, double bass, trumpet and guitar as well as vocals.

Acoustic – played without amplification.

Recorder – a woodwind instrument which dates back to the fourteenth century; there have been several types, tuned to different pitches, but the most common are the descant, treble and bass recorders.

Keyboards (acoustic and electronic; synthesiser) – instruments with playing mechanisms operated from a keyboard. (See Keyboard instruments, page 90.)

Guitars (acoustic and electric) – plucked stringed instruments with frets, normally with six strings. (See Guitars, page 91.)

Fiddle – the word used for a violin when it is used to play certain kinds of music – especially folk music and traditional Scottish music.

Organ – although technically a wind instrument because air produces the sound through large pipes (unless it is a much smaller electric organ), an organ has a keyboard as well as foot pedals and stops (buttons which alter the volume and the type of sound produced).

Drum fill – a passage of drum beats used before the start or at the end of a musical phrase to 'fill' the gaps.

Vocal/choral music – music where voice is the main instrument. Choral music involves a choir (a large group of singers) which can be made up of male voices only, female voices only, male and female voices, or children's voices (youth choir).

Lead vocals – the person who sings the main melody of a song.

Backing vocals – the singers who accompany the lead vocalist.

4: Timbre – General level

In addition to the above Timbre concepts, you should also understand the following:

Indonesian music – music (mainly gamelan music) from the 3000 or more Indonesian archipelago islands (populated by around 300 ethnic groups) which incorporates influences from the Indian, Chinese, Arab and Mongul cultures as well as ancient traditional Indonesian styles.

Gamelan music – a group of musicians from south-east Asia (usually Indonesia) who play their own traditional instruments (gongs, xylophones, metallophones, drums, bowed and plucked strings, oboe, flute) and sing. Gamelan ensembles can range from just a few musicians up to 75, but groups of six singers and 25 players are common. The music is complex and based on a five-note scale (*slendro*) and a seven-note scale (*pelog*) from which various other modes are formed.

Ghanaian drum ensemble – a tribe or group of musicians from Ghana who play lively dance music using various percussion instruments including shakers, finger bells and ankle bells.

Latin percussion group – a group of percussion musicians who play lively Latin dance music.

Voice – the creation of musical notes using the voice, as in songs. For information on the various voice ranges see page 89.

Orchestral, keyboard and folk instruments – see pages 89–91.

Drone – a constantly sustained note (normally a bass note), over which the main melody is played; bagpipes use at least one drone.

Electronic music – music created or altered electronically (using electrical equipment as opposed to the natural acoustic sounds produced by standard instruments). Synthesisers, electric organs and computers using software which enables them to produce sounds all produce electronic music.

Delay – an electronic echo effect used on amplified instruments which repeats the notes or phrases played (or sung) by a musician. The delay time can be adjusted.

Distortion – an electronic effect used on amplified instruments (particularly electric guitar) which creates a 'dirty', distorted sound that is often used in rock and heavy metal music.

Reverb – an electronic effect used to change the acoustic sound of amplified instruments. Reverb can make an instrument sound as though it is in a large concert hall even if it is being played in a small room.

Electric drums – an electronic device (sometimes called a drum machine) which reproduces drum sounds and rhythmic patterns.

4: Timbre – Credit level

In addition to the above Timbre concepts, you should also understand the following:

Vibrato – a technique used by singers and players of stringed instruments where a rapid fluctuation in the pitch of a note is produced, creating the effect that the note is vibrating or swaying gently.

Melismatic – where several notes are sung to a single syllable in vocal music.

Syllabic – where only one note is sung to every syllable in vocal music – the opposite of melismatic music.

Mezzo – 'medium' or 'middle'; for example, mezzo soprano, mezzo forte.

Mezzo-soprano; **counter-tenor**; **baritone** – see page 89.

Con sordino –'with the mute': an instruction to string or brass players to mute their sound.

Flutter-tonguing – a technique used by wind players (especially on the flute) where the tongue rolls the letter 'r' to create a kind of tremolo effect.

Col legno – 'with the wood': an instruction to players of bowed string instruments to play the strings using the wood of the bow – this creates a staccato effect.

Arco – 'bow': an instruction to players of bowed string instruments to go back to playing with the bow after a pizzicato section.

Pizzicato – an instruction to string players to pluck the strings with the fingers instead of using the bow.

Trill – an ornament where two notes a semitone or a tone apart alternate rapidly with each other.

Tremolando/tremolo – the very rapid repetition of a single note to create a trembling effect.

A cappella – a term used to describe unaccompanied choral music.

Chamber music – music for a smaller ensemble (about three to eight players) which is suitable for playing in an indoor room. Typical examples are string or piano trios, quartets and quintets.

Sprechgesang – 'speech song': a vocal technique which is half way between singing and speech; used by twentieth-century composers including Schoenberg and Berg.

5: Texture, Structure and Design – Foundation level

Unison/octave – where all parts in a piece of music sing or play the same notes – either at the same pitch or an octave apart.

Harmony – where notes are combined/played at the same time to produce satisfactory sounds and create texture in a piece of music.

Chord – two or more different notes played at the same time.

Solo – a section of music or a whole piece performed by just one musician.

Ensemble – a group of musicians playing together.

Accompanied – where the most important melody or solo in a piece of music has another instrument or instruments playing along with it (for example, a song with piano accompaniment).

Unaccompanied – where no other instruments play along with the main melody or instrument in a piece of music – opposite to accompanied.

Ostinato – the constant repetition of the same musical phrase, rhythm pattern or chords.

Riff – a short musical phrase of around two to four bars long which is repeated regularly throughout a piece of music (especially in jazz, rock and pop music).

Round – a musical form where all parts consist of the same music begun at staggered intervals to create an overlapping texture (as in the children's song 'Row, Row, Row Your Boat').

Theme and variations – a musical form where a theme is played and then followed by a set of variations based on that theme. The variations may include changes to the speed, key or rhythm of the main theme.

Opera – a musical drama which is performed on stage with scenery (like a play) and singers who wear costumes, act out the roles of particular characters and sing some or all of their parts. The music (probably the most important part of any opera) is played by an orchestra placed in front of and below the stage (the pit). The two main kinds of opera are opera seria (serious opera) and opera buffa (comic opera). Famous opera composers include Mozart, Puccini and Verdi.

Musical – a popular twentieth-century form of musical theatre, developed from comic opera, with lighthearted, romantic or humorous plots and catchy, upbeat songs as well as spectacular dances and spoken text. Composers of musicals include George Gershwin, Stephen Sondheim and Andrew Lloyd Webber.

Overture – an 'introduction': a piece of orchestral music which introduces a big work, especially an opera, and may contain musical features (such as small fragments of tunes) which later appear in the main work.

Hymn tune – a religious devotional song normally sung by church congregations.

Traditional song – an old song which reflects aspects of the culture or traditions of a nation or a community. 'The Bonnie Banks of Loch Lomond' is a traditional Scottish song.

5: Texture, Structure and Design – General level

In addition to the above Texture, Structure and Design concepts, you should also understand the following:

Duet – where two musicians play a piece of music together, each performing different parts.

Improvisation – inventing music on the spot.

Rondo – a musical structure where the main theme (the A section) alternates with several new or contrasting sections of music (for example, ABACADA).

Canon – a musical form where the first melody is imitated by another part (or parts) before the first melody is finished – this creates a texture where tunes overlap each other in a harmonious way.

Binary form – a musical structure, common in baroque music, made up of two main sections, A and B, each of which is usually repeated. The B section is normally longer than the A section.

Ternary form – a musical structure made up of three main sections, ABA, where the B section normally provides some musical contrast and the second A section can either be an exact or altered repeat of the first A section. Sometimes the structure is AABA.

Minuet and trio – a musical structure based on ternary form (ABA) where the A section is the minuet and the B section the trio (a contrasting middle section, usually involving a key change).

Chord – the sounding of two or more notes at the same time; a tonic triad chord is made up of the first, third and fifth notes of a scale (for example, the notes C, E and G make up a C chord).

Arpeggio – a 'broken chord' where the notes of the chord are played one after the other (often in a rhythmic pattern) instead of all together.

Note cluster – a bunch of adjacent notes played together (usually applies to piano music).

Organum – slow-moving religious vocal music from medieval times.

Walking bass – a bass line where the note values and speed remain constant, as though walking steadily; a common technique in baroque music but also used in jazz and boogie-woogie.

Descant – a decorative extra part sung above a melody. It can also refer to an instrument tuned to a particular pitch (as with a descant recorder).

Fanfare – a ceremonial flourish of trumpets or other brass instruments, sometimes with percussion, used for important ceremonies such as royal occasions.

Concerto – a large work, normally in three movements, for a solo instrument and orchestra. Examples are Vivaldi's 'The Four Seasons' (for solo violin and orchestra) and Rodrigo's Concerto de Aranjuez (for solo guitar and orchestra).

Symphony – a large orchestral work, normally in three or four movements, which can last for up to an hour or more. A wide variety of musical structures, keys and emotions are often used in the musical journey of a symphony. Composers of symphonies include Mozart, Beethoven and Mahler.

Slow air – a slow tune or song – in traditional Scottish music this could be sung or played on the bagpipes or fiddle.

Gaelic psalms (or 'long tunes') – religious songs from the Western Isles of Scotland which can be sung slightly differently by individual members of a church congregation, creating an improvised feel.

Scots ballad – a traditional Scottish folk song in which an unfortunate, sad or important historic story is told. (For example, a death, lost love, a disaster, war.)

Bothy ballad – a traditional Scottish folk song about hard work and working conditions (often involving farming).

Pibroch – a term for more serious and complex highland bagpipe music – pibrochs use a theme and variation structure.

Waulking song – a traditional Scottish Gaelic song which was sung by people (mainly women) while they were doing tedious or repetitive work.

Mouth music (port a beul) – an improvised vocal style used in place of musical instruments to accompany Scottish dances.

5: Texture, Structure and Design – Credit level

In addition to the above Texture, Structure and Design concepts, you should also understand the following:

Tierce de Picardie – a technique commonly used in the sixteenth century and in the baroque period where a piece of music in a minor key ends on the major chord (so that, for example, a piece in A minor would finish with an A major chord).

Word painting – a technique used mainly in the sixteenth century and baroque period where music is used to describe the words in a piece of music (for example, the word *misery* could be accompanied by a sad minor chord, or a loud drum might play when the word *thunder* is sung).

Word setting – choosing suitable words to accompany the mood and style of a piece of music.

Tempo – see pages 92–93.

Augmentation – where a passage of music or a melody is repeated in longer note values than when it was first heard.

Diminution – where a passage of music or a melody is repeated in shorter note values than when it was first heard (opposite of augmentation).

Pedal – a note which is held (sustained) or constantly repeated in the bass while other parts above it change.

Inverted pedal – a note which is sustained or constantly repeated in a high part while other parts below it change.

Ground bass – a bass melody or motif which is constantly repeated.

Alberti bass – a broken chord pattern which is used as a bass accompaniment; the pattern is often: *lowest note of chord – highest note of chord – middle note of chord – highest note of chord* (C G E G for a C major chord, for example).

Homophonic – where voices or instruments sounding together move in the same rhythm.

Polyphonic – where two or more voices or instruments sound together but have different rhythms.

Contrapuntal (counterpoint) – where two different musical parts (which sound complete in themselves) are played simultaneously to create a single, harmonious piece – a popular style in the baroque period, but used by composers ever since.

Obbligato – a separate instrumental part which, although secondary to the main melody, must not be left out.

Counter-melody – a second melody which complements the main melody and will usually move in a different rhythm also, as in counterpoint.

Suspension – where a note is held on from a chord to create brief dissonance in the chord which follows, before resolving itself again in the third chord.

Passing note – a note which appears in between two notes (normally a third apart) to create a smooth, stepwise movement (thus, the note D would be a passing note between C and E to produce C *D* E).

Suite (related pieces, not dance suites) – a selection of pieces taken from a large work such as an opera, or a collection of pieces that are related to each other in some way.

Fugue – a musical form where a main theme is developed and extended through different kinds of imitation.

Sonata – a musical structure with three main sections: the first section (the exposition) introduces the main musical themes; the second section (the development) develops these themes in various keys and the third section (the recapitulation) re-states the themes of the first section (with some key variation). The sonata was the most important musical structure in the classical period.

Scherzo – a lively, playful instrumental movement which is usually part of a larger work such as a sonata or symphony and is often accompanied by a trio section.

Cantata – a large vocal work (often religious) for chorus and orchestra, especially popular in the baroque period.

Oratorio – a large musical setting of a religious text involving choir, soloists and orchestra; similar to opera, but without acting, costumes or scenery.

Chorale – a congregational hymn tune of the Lutheran (German) church. Composers such as J. S. Bach built more complex pieces of music around these basic hymn tunes.

Recitative – a speech in an opera which is sung in a way which follows the natural pitch and rhythms of spoken words (creating a kind of half-sung half-spoken effect).

Aria – a song, especially from an opera.

Chorus – a large group of singers who perform together, often divided into parts for different voice ranges.

Programme music – music which describes a particular scene, emotion or story (such as a stormy sea, rainfall, a biblical story or a person's death).

Strophic – a term used to describe vocal music in which different lyrics are sung to the same musical verse each time.

Through-composed – a term used to describe a song where the music changes in each verse or stanza, or a piece of music with no definite form.

Quartet – a group of four musicians or a piece of music written for such a group.

Coda – a short 'ending' section which concludes a piece of music.

Cadenza – a complex section for the soloist (which shows his/her skill) near the end of a concerto movement or an aria.

Serial – a section of music or a whole piece which uses serialism (see serialism, page 105) in its composition.

6: Harmony – Foundation level

Recognition of chord change – the ability to recognise (with your ear) when a chord has changed in a piece of music.

6: Harmony – General level

In addition to the above Harmony concepts, you should also understand the following:

Recognition of specific chord changes – the ability to recognise (with your ear) chord changes between chords I, IV and V in major keys.

Tonality – identifying whether a piece of music is in a major or minor key.

Simple blues/rock progression – typical chord progressions (using chords I, IV and V) in blues and rock music.

6: Harmony – Credit level

In addition to the above Harmony concepts, you should also understand the following:

Recognition of specific chord changes – the ability to recognise (with your ear) chord changes between chords I, IV, V and VI in major and minor keys.

Basic awareness of cadence – the ability to recognise perfect and imperfect cadences

Discord/dissonance – notes or chords which sound harsh or out of tune.

Basic awareness of modulation – the ability to recognise the precise point when a piece of music changes key.

7: Dynamics – Foundation level

Pianissimo (*pp*) – very quiet.

Piano (*p*) – quiet.

Mezzo piano (*mp*) – moderately quiet.

Mezzo forte (*mf*) – moderately loud.

Forte (*f*) – loud.

Fortissimo (*ff*) – very loud.

Crescendo (*cresc.*) – becoming louder.

Diminuendo (*dim.*) – becoming quieter.

7: Dynamics – General level

In addition to the above Dynamics concepts, you should also understand the following:

Methods of achieving dynamic gradation – changing dynamics (volume) by adding or subtracting musical instruments.

7: Dynamics – Credit level

The requirements for Credit level are the same as for Foundation and General level combined.

ANSWERS TO EXERCISES IN CHAPTERS 1 AND 2

Chapter 1: Revising musical concepts

Concepts 1: Melody – Foundation level

CD track 1

Question 1

☑ Moving by step

☑ Ascending

Question 2

☑ TRUE

CD track 2

Question 1

☑ Question and Answer

Question 2

☑ Broken chords

Concepts 1: Melody – General level

CD track 3

Question 1

☑ Imitation

Question 2

☑ Minor

Concepts 1: Melody – Credit level

CD track 4

Question 1

☑ Tonal

Question 2

☑ The melody is in a **high register**

Question 3

☑ The music modulates from the **major key** into its **relative minor** key

Question 4

☑ The accompaniment moves in CONTRARY MOTION

Concepts 2: Rhythm – Foundation level

CD track 5

Question 1

☑ Two beats in the bar

Question 2

☑ March

CD track 6

Question 1

☑ The accent is on the beat

Question 2

☑ Repetition

Concepts 2: Rhythm – General level

CD track 7

Question 1

☑ The excerpt is in SIMPLE TIME

Question 2

☑ Anacrusis

☑ Scotch snap

CD track 8

Question 1

☑ Sometimes the downbeats are accented, and sometimes the upbeats are accented

Question 2

☑ Ritardando (*rit.*)

Concepts 2: Rhythm – Credit level

CD track 9

Question 1

☑ 4/4 time (simple time)

Question 2

☑ The music moves mostly in QUAVERS and SEMIQUAVERS

Question 3

☑ TRUE

Concepts 3: Style – Foundation level

CD track 10

Question 1

☑ Blues

CD track 11

Question 1

☑ Reggae

Concepts 3: Style – General level

CD track 12

Question 1

☑ Salsa

Question 2

☑ FALSE

CD track 13

Question 1

☑ Brass and percussion instruments have an important role in the orchestra

☑ The mood or emotion is expressed very powerfully

Question 2

☑ TRUE

Concepts 3: Style – Credit level

CD track 14

Question 1

☑ Gospel

CD track 15

Question 1

☑ Classical

CD track 16

Question 1

☑ Atonal

Concepts 4: Timbre – Foundation level

CD track 17

Question 1

☑ Jazz group

Question 2

☑ Trumpet

Question 3

☑ The melody is played LEGATO

CD track 18

Question 1

☑ Big band

Question 2

☑ Blowing

Concepts 4: Timbre – General level

CD track 19

Question 1

☑ Latin percussion group

Question 2

☑ Flute

Question 3

☑ Trumpet

Concepts 4: Timbre – Credit level

CD track 20

Question 1

☑ Syllabic

Question 2

☑ Soprano

Question 3

☑ Trill

Concepts 5: Texture, Structure and Design – Foundation level

CD track 21

Question 1

☑ Voices in harmony

Question 2

☑ Unaccompanied

CD track 22

Question 1

☑ Musical

Question 2

☑ TRUE

Concepts 5: Texture, Structure and Design – General level

CD track 23

Question 1

☑ Organum

Question 2

☑ Descant

Concepts 5: Texture, Structure and Design – Credit level

CD track 24

Question 1

☑ Chorus

☑ Strophic

Question 2

☑ Aria

CD track 25

Question 1

☑ Fugue

Question 2

☑ Counterpoint

Concepts 6: Harmony – Foundation level

CD track 26

Question 1

INTRODUCTION

      X   X   X   X

Shine on Ruby Mountain, from the valley to the sea.

       X   X   X   X

Shine on Ruby Mountain, shine your sweet love down on me.

Concepts 6: Harmony – General level

CD track 27

Question 1

INTRODUCTION

Goin' back to Kansas City, Kansas City here I come.

Goin' back to Kansas City, Kansas City here I come, yeah

                    (I / E♭)

I'm gonna find my baby and we're gonna have some fun.

Question 2

☑ The tonality is MAJOR

Concepts 6: Harmony – Credit level

CD track 28

Question 1

Everybody's looking for that something, one thing that makes it all complete.

You find it in the strangest places, places you never knew it could be.

Some find it in the face of their children, some find it in their lover's eyes

IV
D

V
E

Who can deny the joy it brings, you've found that special thing,

I
A

You're flying without wings.

Question 2

☑ Imperfect cadence

Concepts 7: Dynamics – Foundation level

 CD track 29

Question 1

☑ *pp* (pianissimo)

Question 2

☑ Diminuendo

Chapter 2: Listening

Sample Listening test paper – Foundation level

Section I
Question 1

 CD track 30

This piece is played by <u>A FOLK GROUP</u>

Question 2

CD track 31

☑ Instruments

Question 3

CD track 32

☑ FALSE

Question 4

CD track 33

☑ Mainly by LEAP

Question 5

CD track 34

☑ There are FOUR beats in a bar

☑ TRUE

Question 6

CD track 35

COLUMN A   COLUMN B

☑ Plucking   ☑ Solo

Question 7

CD track 36

             X
As morning breaks, the heaven on high

X   X
I lift my heavy load to the skies

X   X
Sun come down with a burning glow

X   X
Mingles my sweat with the earth below

X   X
Oh island in the sun

X   X
Willed to me by my father's hand

X   X
All my days I will sing in praise

      X   X
Of your forest water, your shining sun.

Section II
Question 8

CD track 37

This is an example of <u>ROCK 'N' ROLL</u>

Question 9

CD track 38

This is an example of a <u>WALTZ</u>

A lead-in is present ☑ TRUE

Question 10

CD track 39

COLUMN A	COLUMN B
☑ Voices in unison/octaves	☑ Accompanied

Question 11

CD track 40

A SEQUENCE is present ☑ FALSE

Question 12

CD track 41

The music is played by the <u>BRASS</u>

Sample Listening test paper – General level

Section I
Question 1

CD track 42

☑ Pipe band

Question 2 (a)

CD track 43

☑ Ostinato   ☑ Electric drums

Question 2 (b)

CD track 44

COLUMN A	COLUMN B
☑ Electric guitar	☑ Staccato melody

Question 2 *(c)*

☑ Repetition   ☑ Riff

Question 2 *(d)*

CD track 45

☑ Electric guitar   ☑ Synthesiser

Question 2 *(e)*

CD track 46

☑ Arpeggios

Question 3 *(a)*

CD track 47

☑ Jig

Question 3 *(b)*

CD track 48

☑ Mouth music

Question 4 *(a)*

CD track 49

☑ Violin

Question 4 *(b)*

CD track 50

☑ Sequence   ☑ Sforzando

Question 4 *(c)*

CD track 51

☑ Pizzicato   ☑ Imitation

Question 5

CD track 52

INTRODUCTION

I		IV		I		IV
C		F		C		F

Someday I'm gonna write the story of my life;

I		V		IV		V
C		G		F		G

I'll tell about the night we met and how my heart can't forget

I		IV	V	I
C		F	G	C

The way you smiled at me.

Section II
Question 6 *(a)*

CD track 53

☑ Ragtime

Question 6 *(b)*

☑ Four beats in a bar

Question 7 *(a)*

CD track 54

☑ Tenor

Question 7 *(b)*

CD track 55

☑ Saxophone

Question 7 *(c)*

☑ Vamp

Question 8 *(a)*

CD track 56

☑ Latin percussion ensemble

Question 8 *(b)*

☑ Flute   ☑ Improvisation

Question 8 *(c)*

CD track 57

☑ Minor key

Question 8 *(d)*

☑ Walking bass   ☑ Organ

Question 9 *(a)*

CD track 58

☑ Concerto

Question 9 *(b)*

CD track 59

☑ Symphony

Question 9 *(c)*

CD track 60

☑ Opera

Sample Listening test paper – Credit level

Section I
Question 1 *(a)*

CD track 61

☑ Baroque

Question 1 *(b)*

☑ Melismatic   ☑ Imitation   ☑ Polyphony

Question 1 *(c)*

CD track 62

☑ Pedal

Question 1 *(d)*

CD track 63

COLUMN A	COLUMN B
☑ Reggae	☑ Syncopation

Question 2 *(a)*

CD track 64

☑ Folk	☑ Three beats per bar

Question 2 *(b)*

☑ Arpeggios

Question 3

CD track 65

I		V		VI
G		D		Em

...I'm loving angels instead.   And through it all she offers me protection

IV		I
C		G

A lot of love and affection, whether I'm right or wrong.

V		VI
D		Em

And down the waterfall   wherever it may take me,

IV		I
C		G

I know that life won't break   me when I come to call ...

Question 4

CD track 66

Musical Aspect	Musical means and effect created
Rhythm/tempo	2. The tempo slows down briefly just after a passage played by staccato trumpets and electric guitar; this is followed by a crescendo where electric guitar has the melody (which builds the drama), taking us into a faster section with a more regular tempo where drums keep the beat. This whole section suggests an increase in the ship's speed.
Melody/harmony	4. Sequences of fast, descending scale-like passages (a little like glissandi) played on electric guitar suggest water breaking over the ship's bow – they also suggest that the ship is pitching gently up and down in the water.
Orchestration	Unison trumpets. Electric guitar. Drums. Synthesisers. 1. Loud accented drum beats (accompanied by synthesisers) suggest the power of the turning propellers disturbing the water's surface. 3. Two different synthesised sounds suggest the ship's foghorn/siren.
Dynamics	There are no particularly quiet sections, but different instrumental combinations provide dynamic contrast, making the music louder in some areas than it is in others. The overall dynamic effect is that the music has been steadily building towards the section near the end of the excerpt where the tempo becomes more regular with drums beating time.

Section II
Question 5 *(a)*

CD track 67

☑ Pedal ☑ Pizzicato

Question 5 *(b)*

☑ Sequence ☑ Trill

Question 5 *(c)*

☑ Major

Question 5 *(d)*

CD track 68

COLUMN A	COLUMN B	COLUMN C
☑ Minor	☑ Tremolo	☑ Oboe

Question 5 *(e)*

The cadence at the end of the excerpt is <u>a perfect cadence</u>

Question 6

CD tracks 69 and 70

	Version one	*Version two*
Instruments and how they are used	Trumpet played staccato at start, imitated by horns	Electric guitar at start (melody played more legato than version one), imitated by unison electric guitars
	Timpani	
	Ostinato strings, staccato strings, strings playing sequences, pizzicato bass strings	Bodhran/drum effects
		Acoustic guitar
		Bass guitar
		Synthesiser
	Woodwind imitates melody first played by strings	Sleigh bells
		Mandolin
	Cymbals	
		Electric guitar plays the main melody throughout
	Big dynamic contrast: **p** (piano) to **ff** (fortissimo)	
		Similar dynamic throughout
Rhythm/tempo	Fast, lively tempo; *vivace* or *allegro*	Slower tempo; *moderato*
Tonality	Major key at start of excerpt. Brief modulations to a minor key take place.	Similar tonal structure to version one

Question 7 *(a)*

CD track 71

☑ Cross rhythms   ☑ Inverted pedal

Question 7 *(b)*

CD track 72

☑ Impressionism   ☑ Rubato

Question 7 *(c)*

CD track 73

☑ Arpeggios   ☑ Contrary motion

Question 8

CD track 74

INTRODUCTION

5

You've painted up your lips and rolled and curled your tinted hair

Ruby are you contemplating going out somewhere

The shadow on the wall tells me the sun is going down

1   3   2

Oh Ruby   **don't take your love to town.**

4

It wasn't me that started that old crazy Asian war

6

But I was proud to go and do my patriotic chore.

CD TRACK LIST

CD track	Title	Composer (Performers)	Recording Co.	Page
1	Revision example 1	Joe McGowan	Hodder Gibson	7
2	Revision example 2	Joe McGowan	Hodder Gibson	7–8
3	Revision example 3	Joe McGowan	Hodder Gibson	8–9
4	Revision example 4	Joe McGowan	Hodder Gibson	9–10
5	2/4 march	Trad. (The Graham Laurie Accordion Orchestra)	KRL CDLOC 1087	10–11
6	'Spring' (The Four Seasons)	Vivaldi (Salzburg Baroque Orchestra)	New sound 2000 Ltd NST 176	11
7	Hebridean Schottische	John MacLeod (arr. A. MacCuish / Hunter)	Ros Dubh Records SKYECD 18	12
8	Dance of the Swans (Swan Lake)	Tchaikovsky (London Festival Orchestra)	POINT Entertainment Ltd UC 1502	12
9	'Ceilidh Carribea'	Trad. (arr. A. MacCuish / D. Gracie)	Ros Dubh Records RD 001	13
10	'Three O'clock Blues'	BB King	Proper Records Ltd INTROCD 2022	14
11	'My Bride To Be'	Winston Samuels	Trojan Records TRBCD 014Z -UK	14
12	'Prestame Tu Mujer'	Ray Barretto	Charly Records Ltd CDHOT 518	15
13	1812 Overture	Tchaikowsky (London Symphony Orchestra)	New sound 2000 Ltd NST 175	15
14	'Heaven On My Mind'	The Original Five Blind Boys of Alabama	Ace Records Ltd CDCHD 479	16
15	Eine Kleine Nachtmusik	Mozart (Hamburg Symphony Orchestra)	New sound 2000 Ltd NST 174	16
16	Revision example 16	Joe McGowan	Hodder Gibson	17
17	'Tin Tin Deo'	Ray Barretto	Charly Records Ltd CDHOT 518	18
18	'Sepian Bounce'	Ken Burns (Jay McShann and his orchestra)	The Verve Music Group 549 084-2	18–19

CD track	Title	Composer (Performers)	Recording Co.	Page
19	'Baila Como Es'	Tito Puente	RCA Recordings (74321 874722)	19–20
20	'Behold the Lamb of God' (Messiah)	Handel (Royal Philharmonic Orchestra)	EMI Records Roy 6430	21
21	'The Shepherd of the Downs'	Peter Bellamy	Topic Records TSCD4001-2	22
22	'One Day More' (Les Misérables)	Alain Boublil & Claude-Michel Schönberg	First Night Records Encore CD1	22
23	Vittoria Kyrie	Traditional	Music Collection International MCCD 1	23–24
24	'L'amour est un oiseau rebelle' (Carmen)	Bizet (Teresa Berganza; The Ambrosian Singers; The London Symphony Orchestra)	Universal 469 630-2	25
25	Fugue for two Harpsichords	J. S. Bach (Karl Munchinger)	Decca 467267-2	25
26	'Shine On Ruby Mountain'	Kenny Rogers	Dressed To Kill METRO 390	26
27	'Hey! Hey! Hey! Hey!'	The Johnny Otis Orchestra	Ace Records CDCHD 774	27–28
28	'Flying Without Wings'	Steve Mac and Wayne Hector (Evelyn Laurie)	Laurie Music	28–29
29	Enigma Variations (Nimrod)	Elgar (London Symphony Orchestra)	New sound 2000 Ltd NST 175	30
30	'Spiral Staircase'	Ralph McTell	Topic Records TSCD 4001-1	33
31	'El Pito'	Joe Cuba	Soul Jazz Records SJR CD45	33
32	L'Arlésienne Suite no. 2 (Farandole)	Bizet (French National Radio Orchestra)	New sound 2000 Ltd NST 174	33
33	Te Deum	Charpentier (London Festival Orchestra)	New sound 2000 Ltd NST 176	33
34	Horn Concerto no. 4	Mozart (Baroque Ensemble of Vienna)	New sound 2000 Ltd NST 176	33–34
35	'Spanish Romance'	Anon. (Joe McGowan)	Casa Tegoyo	34
36	'Island In The Sun'	(The Spinners)	Kaz Records PLS CD158	34

CD track	Title	Composer (Performers)	Recording Co.	Page
37	'At My Front Door'	The Jayos	Ace Records Ltd CDCHD 774	35
38	Gaelic Waltz	Trad. (arr. A. MacCuish / D. Gracie)	Ros Dubh Records RD 001	35
39	'Voici la cloche qui sonne, mon lieutenant' (Carmen)	Bizet (Placido Domingo; The Ambrosian Singers; The London Symphony Orchestra)	Universal 469 630-2	35
40	Orpheus in the Underworld Overture	Offenbach (Royal Philharmonic Orchestra)	New sound 2000 Ltd NST 174	36
41	Pictures at an Exhibition	Mussorgsky (Russian State Symphony Orchestra)	New sound 2000 Ltd NST 174	36
42	'Old Toastie'	Trad.	CMR Records PACD 031	36
43	'Old Field, New Age'	Joe McGowan	Star Studios	37
44	'Groove Axis'	David Brockett	Star Studios	37
45	'Old Field, New Age'	Joe McGowan	Star Studios	37
46	'Heaven's Gate'	David Brockett	Star Studios	38
47	Jig	Trad. (The Graham Laurie Accordion Orchestra)	KRL CDLOC 1087	38
48	'Look at Ewen's Coracle'	Trad. (Annie Arnott)	Greentrax Records	38
49	Violin Concerto no. 1 in G minor	Bruch (Kiev Philharmonia)	New sound 2000 Ltd NST 174	38
50	The Barber of Seville Overture	Rossini (Munich Symphony Orchestra)	New sound 2000 Ltd NST 176	39
51	Symphony no. 8 (Unfinished) (first movement)	Schubert (Hamburg Symphony Orchestra)	New sound 2000 Ltd NST 174	39
52	'The Story Of My Life'	(Gary Miller)	Kaz Records PLS CD 158	39
53	The Sycamore Rag	Scott Joplin (Joe McGowan)	Hodder Gibson	40
54	'Monsieur le Brigadier?' (Carmen)	Bizet (Placido Domingo; The London Symphony Orchestra)	Universal 469 630-2	40
55	'Rockin' At Home'	Floyd Dixon	El Toro Records DOCK 509.03000.02	40–41

CD track	Title	Composer (Performers)	Recording Co.	Page
56	'Asi Es Como Era (Malibu)'	Tito Puente	RCA Recordings 74321 874 722	41
57	Adagio for Strings and Organ	Albinoni (Baroque Ensemble of Vienna)	New sound 2000 Ltd NST 174	41
58	Piano Concerto in F major (first movement)	George Gershwin (Dieter Goldman; Philharmonica Slavonica)	Hallmark Classical HALMCD 1054	42
59	Fifth Symphony (Trauermarsch)	Mahler (Austrian Radio Symphony Orchestra)	New sound 2000 Ltd	42
60	'Voici la cloche qui sonne, mon lieutenant' (Carmen)	Bizet (Placido Domingo; The Ambrosian Singers; The London Symphony Orchestra)	Universal 469 630-2	42
61	'For unto us a child is born' (Messiah)	Handel (Royal Philharmonic Orchestra)	EMI Records Roy 6430	43
62	Javert's Suicide: soliloquy (Les Misérables)	Alain Boublil & Claude-Michel Schönberg	First Night Records Encore CD2	43
63	'Mattie Rag (AKA Ol' Matilda)'	Lord Tanamo	Trojan Records TRBCD 014Z -UK	43
64	'The Rose of Allandale'	Bandoggs	Topic Records TSCD 4001-2	44
65	'Angels'	Robbie Williams/Guy Chambers (Evelyn Laurie)	Laurie Music	44–45
66	QE2	Mike Oldfield	Virgin Records Ltd 7243 8 49377 2 0	45
67	Giselle	Adam (Nuremberg Symphony Orchestra)	POINT Entertainment Ltd UC 1502	47
68	Dance of the Swans (Swan Lake)	Tchaikowsky (London Festival Orchestra)	POINT Entertainment Ltd UC 1502	47–48
69	William Tell Overture	Rossini (Royal Philharmonic Orchestra)	New sound 2000 Ltd NST 174	48
70	William Tell Overture	Rossini (Mike Oldfield)	Virgin Records Ltd CDMOC 1	48
71	Hungarian Rhapsody	Liszt (Rhapsody Royal Danish Symphony Orchestra)	New sound 2000 Ltd NST 174	50

CD track	Title	Composer (Performers)	Recording Co.	Page
72	'Clair de lune'	Debussy (Nicholas York)	New sound 2000 Ltd NST 175	50
73	Liebestraum no. 3	Liszt (Royal Danish Symphony Orchestra)	New sound 2000 Ltd NST 176	50
74	'Ruby (Don't Take Your Love To Town)'	Kenny Rogers	Dressed To Kill METRO 390	51
75	'From the Dungeon'	Joe McGowan	Hodder Gibson	64
76	Study in A	Joe McGowan	Hodder Gibson	75–76
77	Lullaby	Joe McGowan	Hodder Gibson	81–82